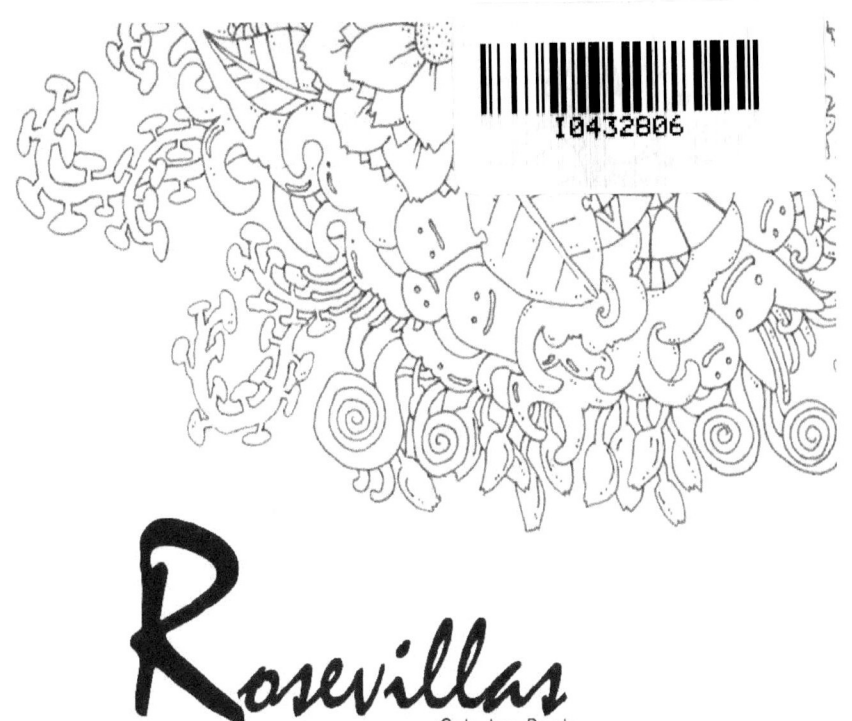

Rosevillas
Coloring Book

Hand Drawn Illustrations

By

Lorie Dinorog

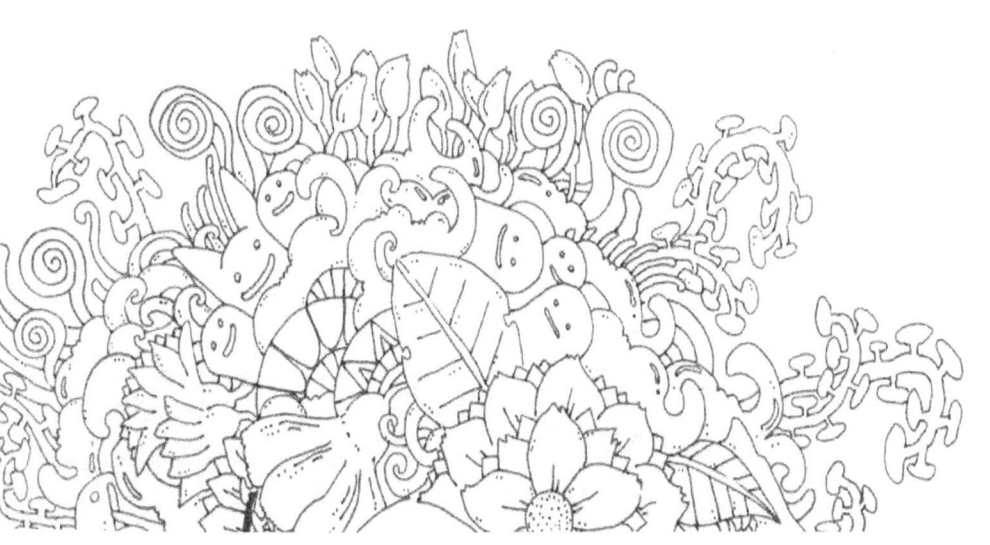

Copyright © 2017 Lorie Dinorog
All rights reserved.
ISBN 10: 1975734777
ISBN-13: 978-1975734770

Instagram.com/Loriedinorog

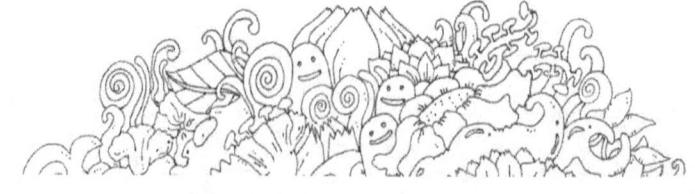

This book
Is dedicated
To the kindest,
Most forgiving,
Patiently loving,
And fairest of them all!

"*Rosevilla*"

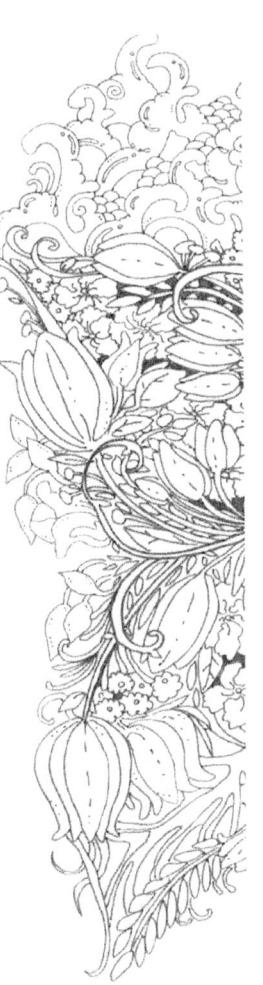

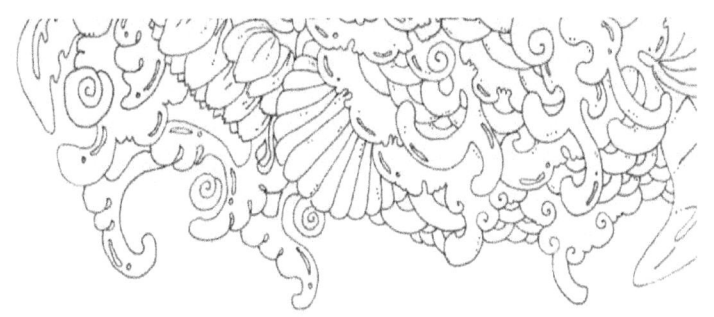

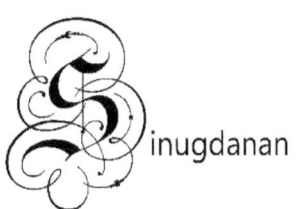inugdanan

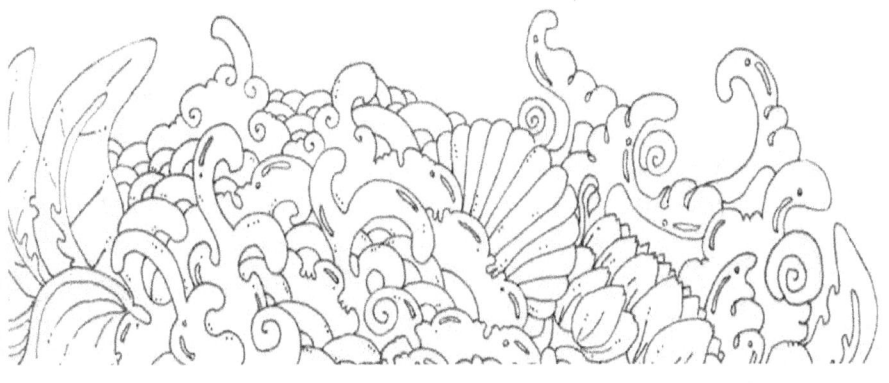

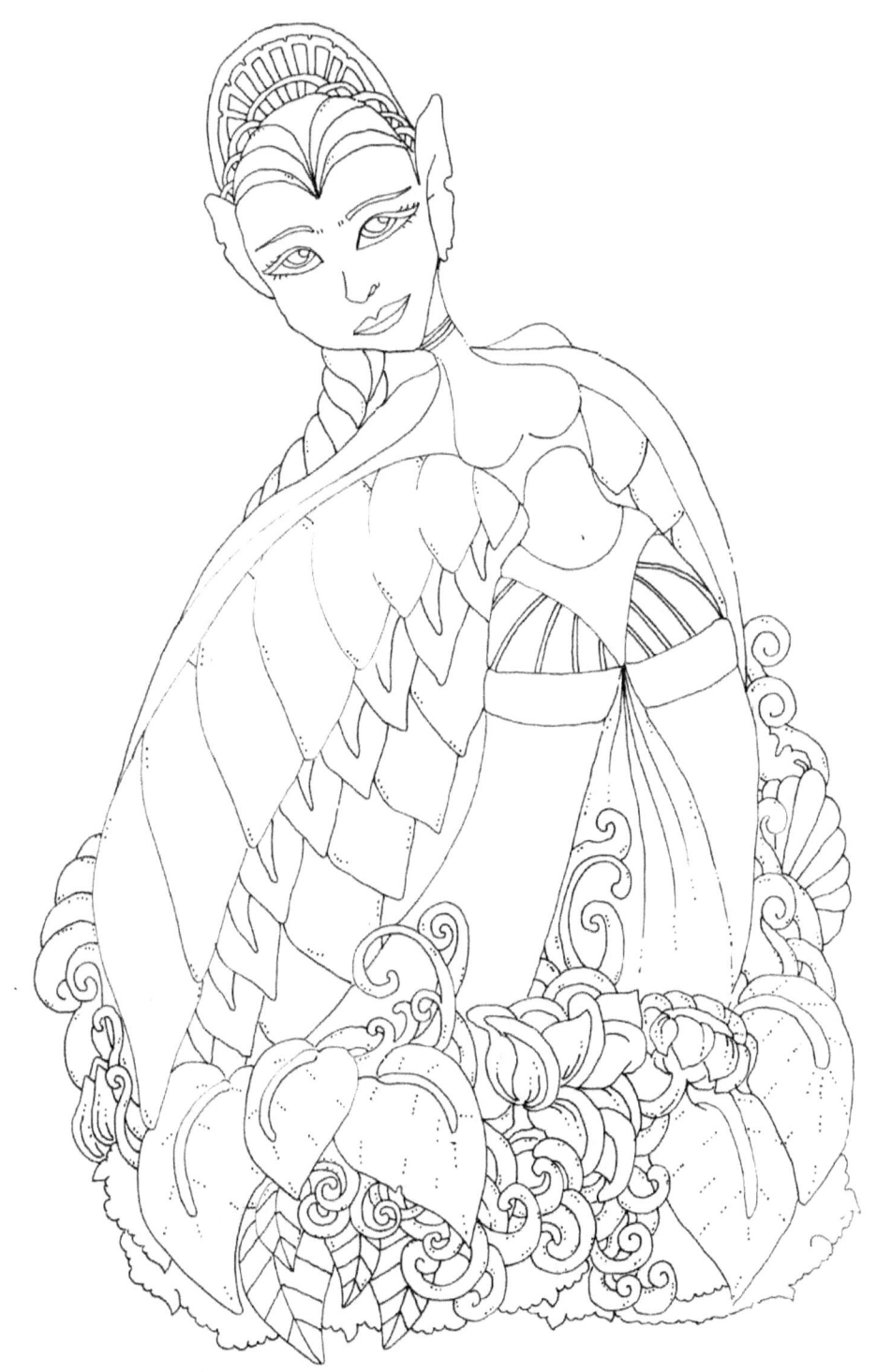

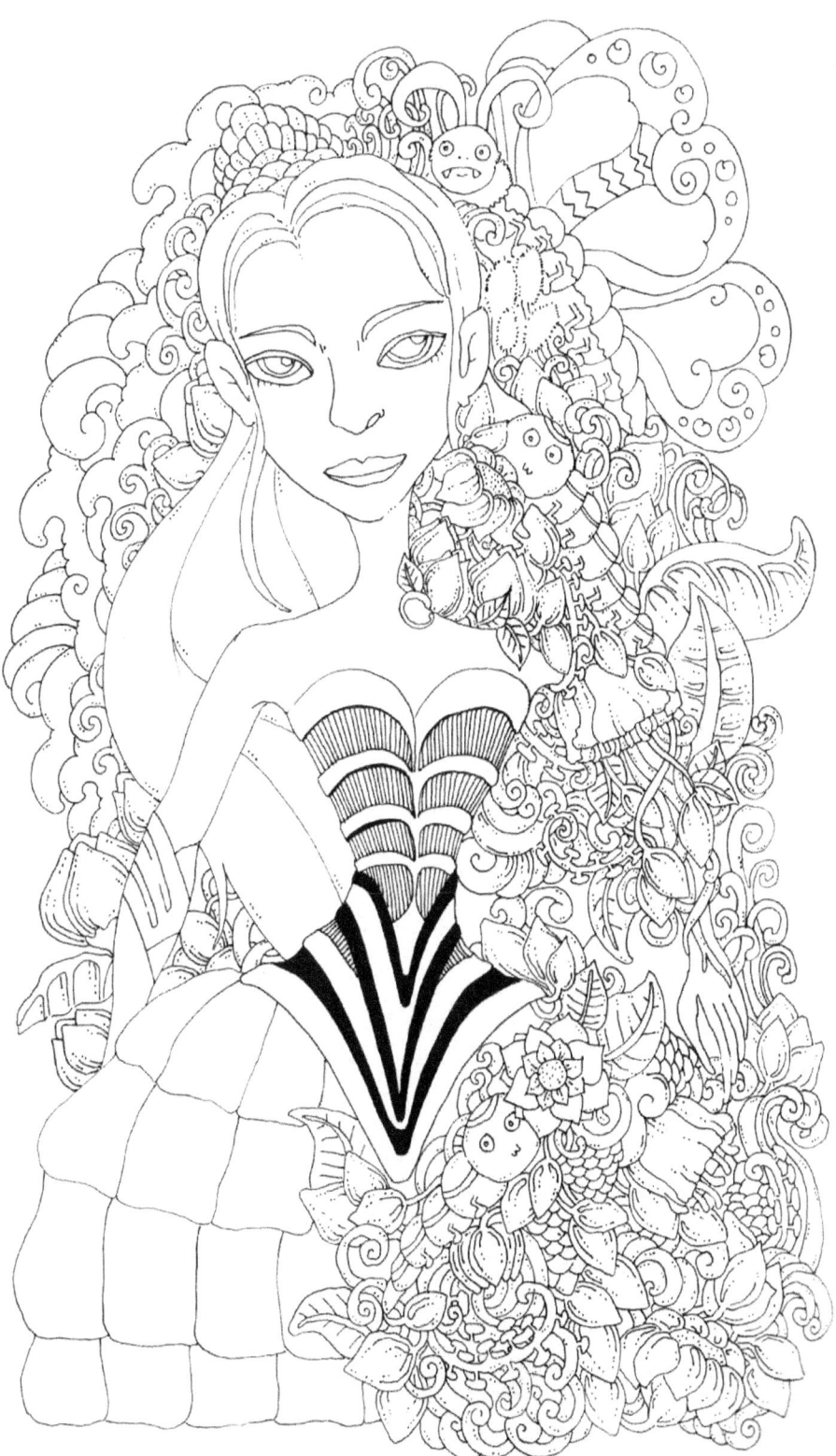

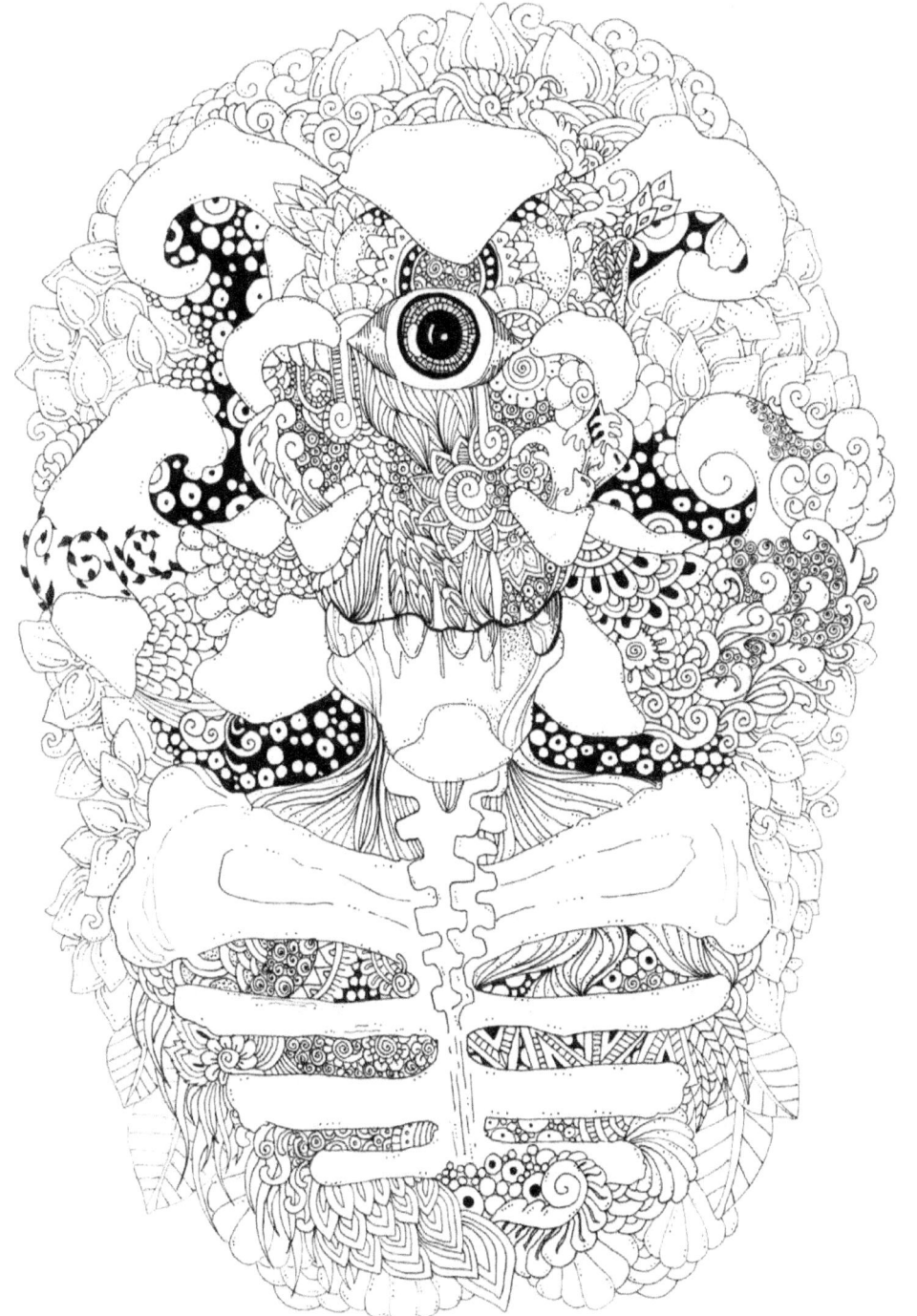

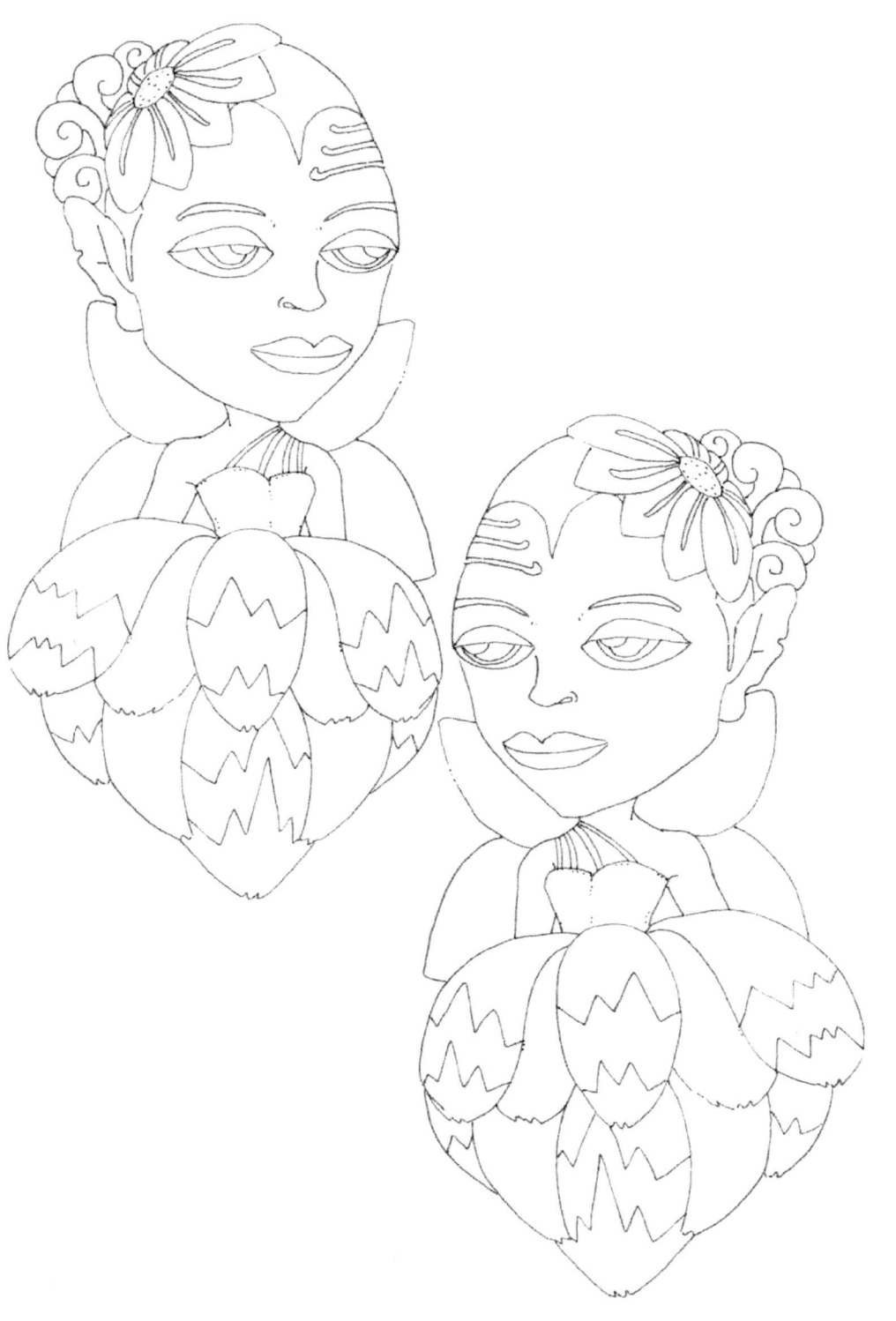

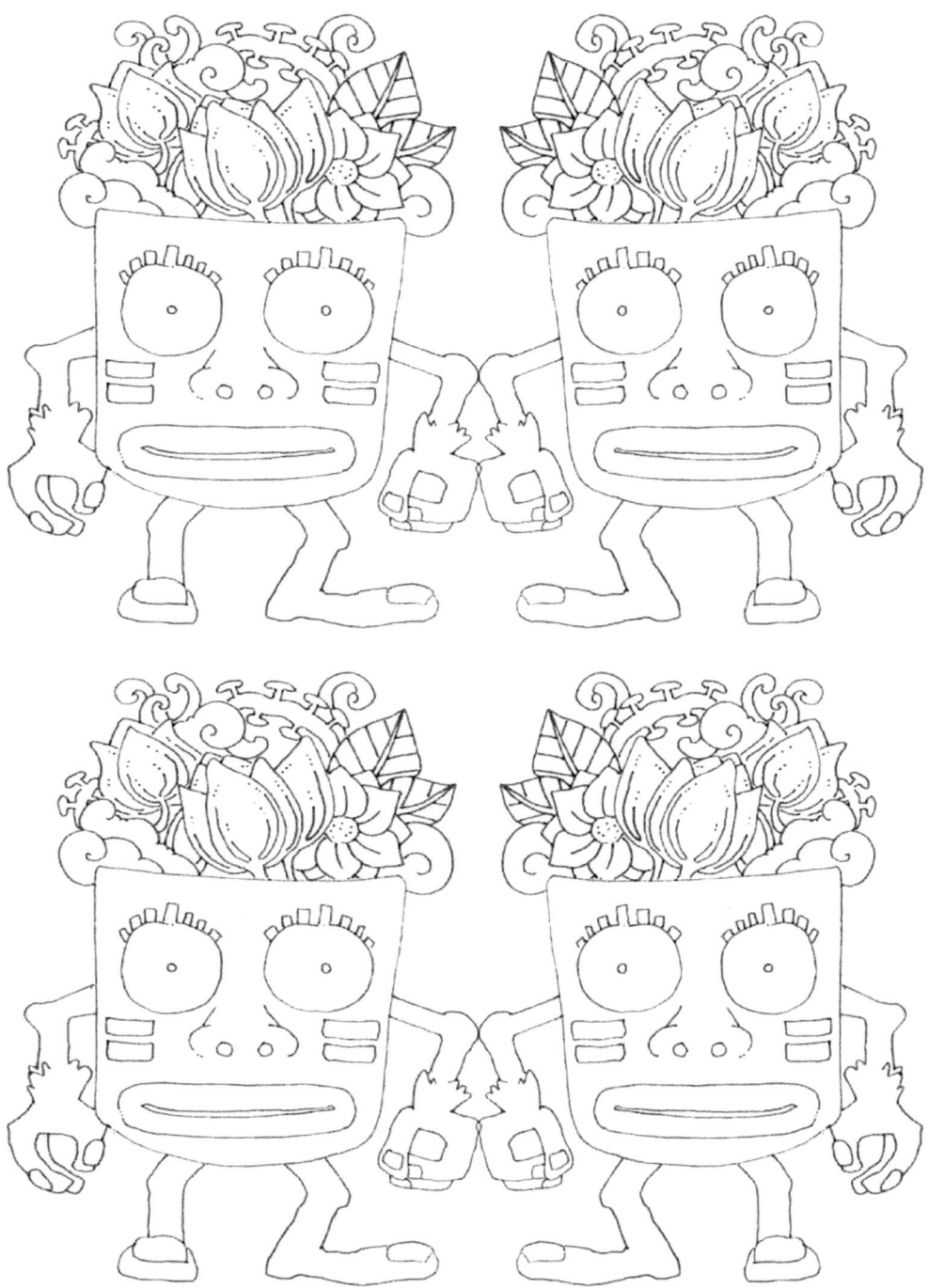

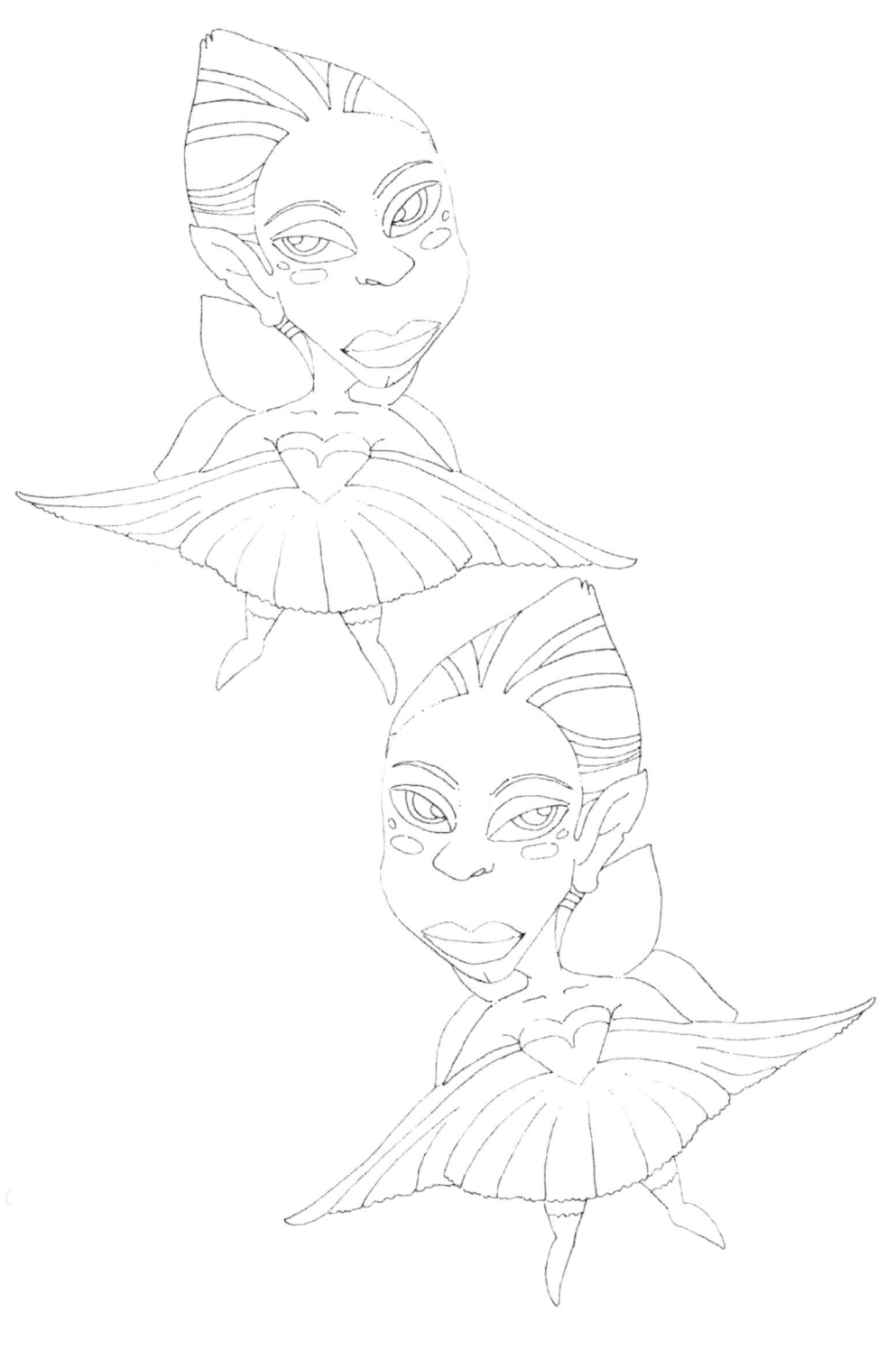

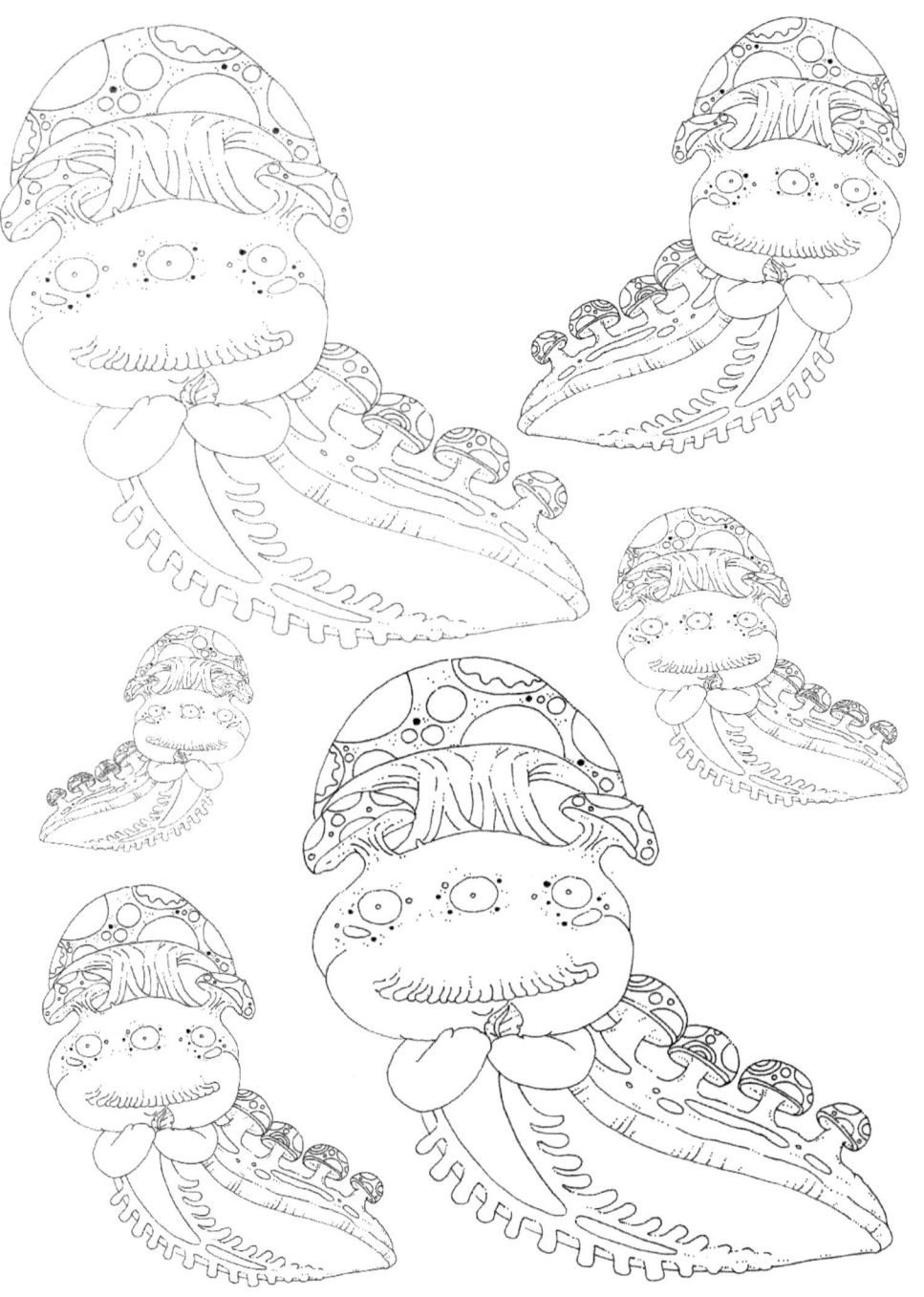

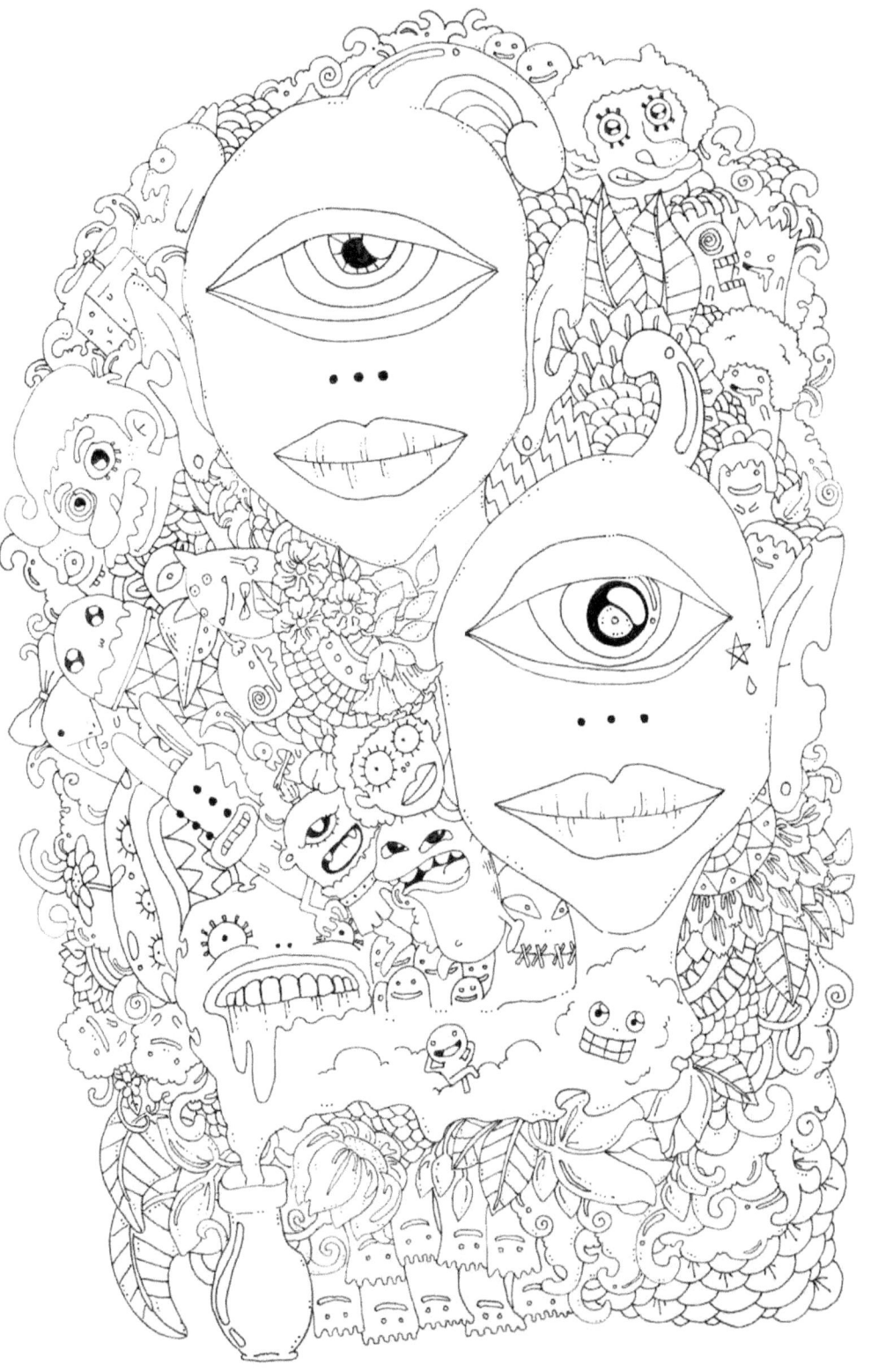

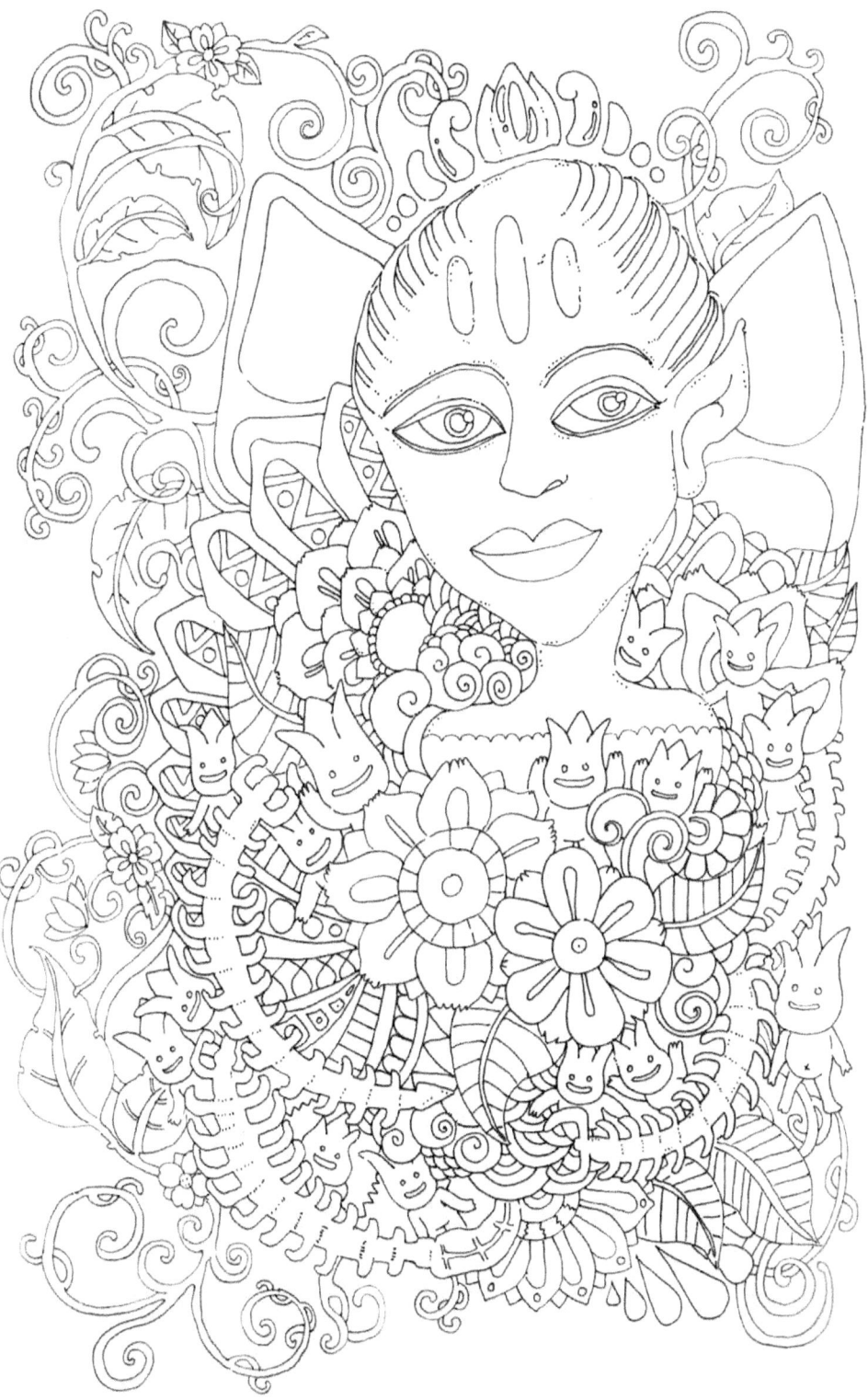

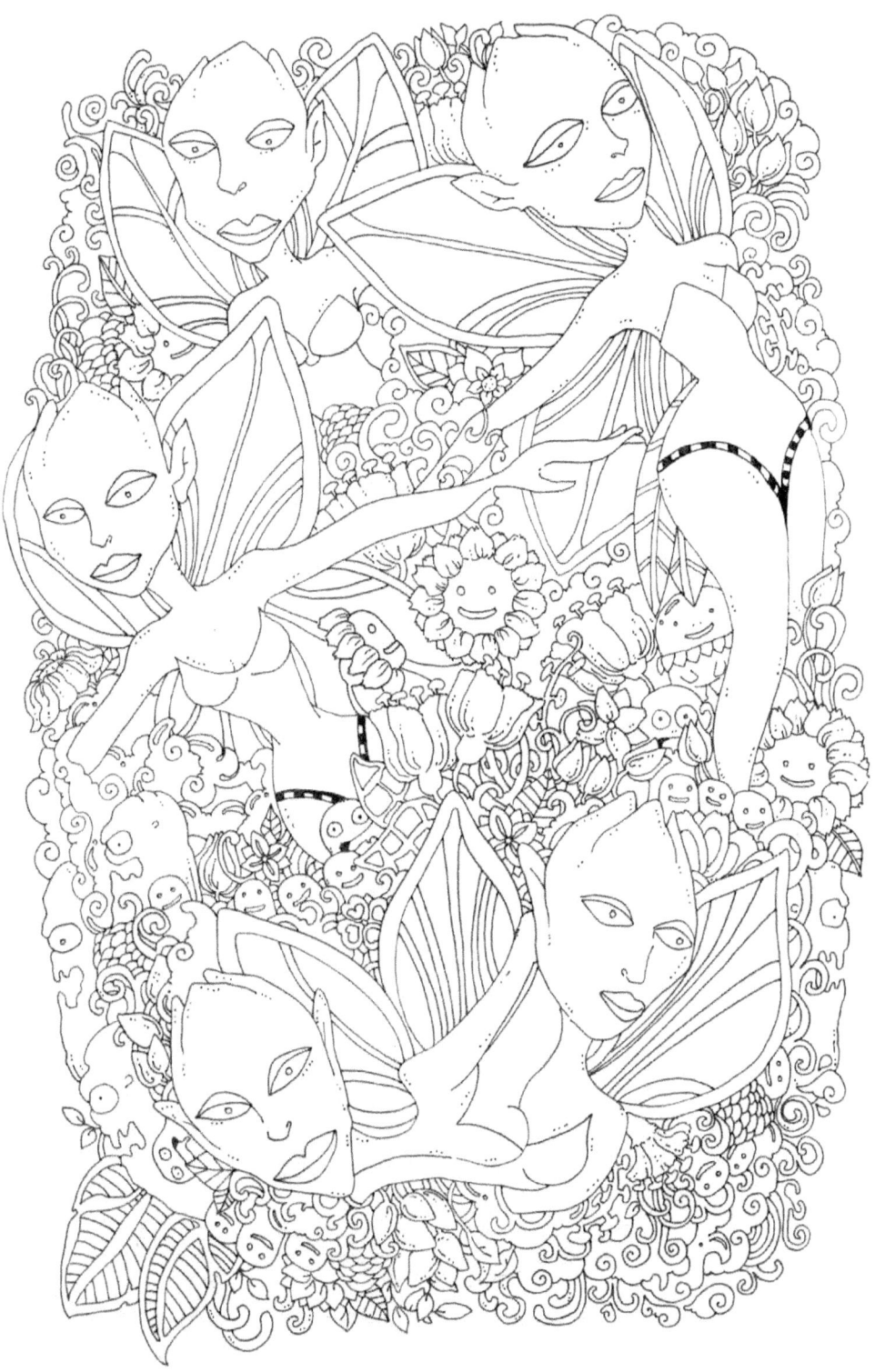

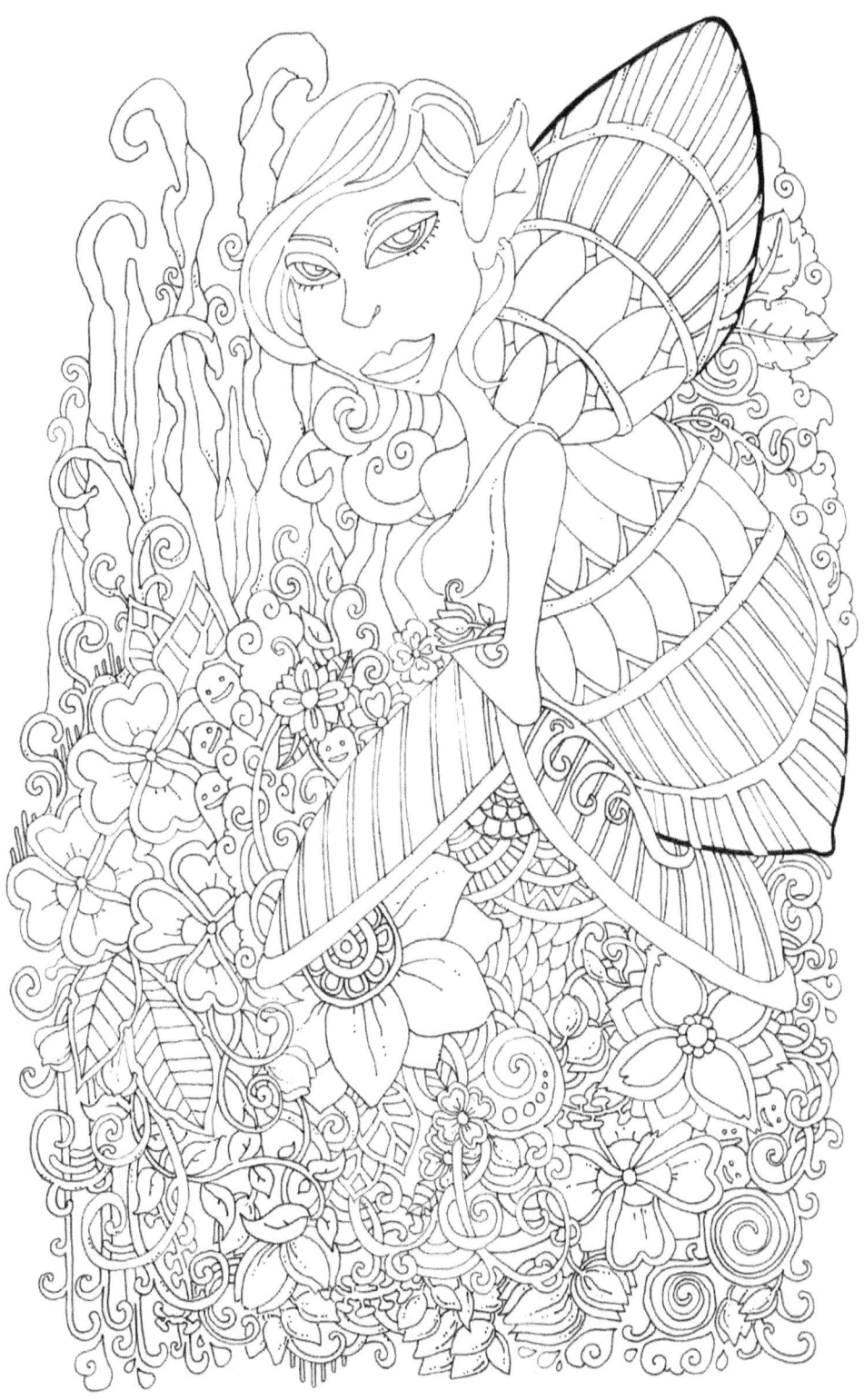

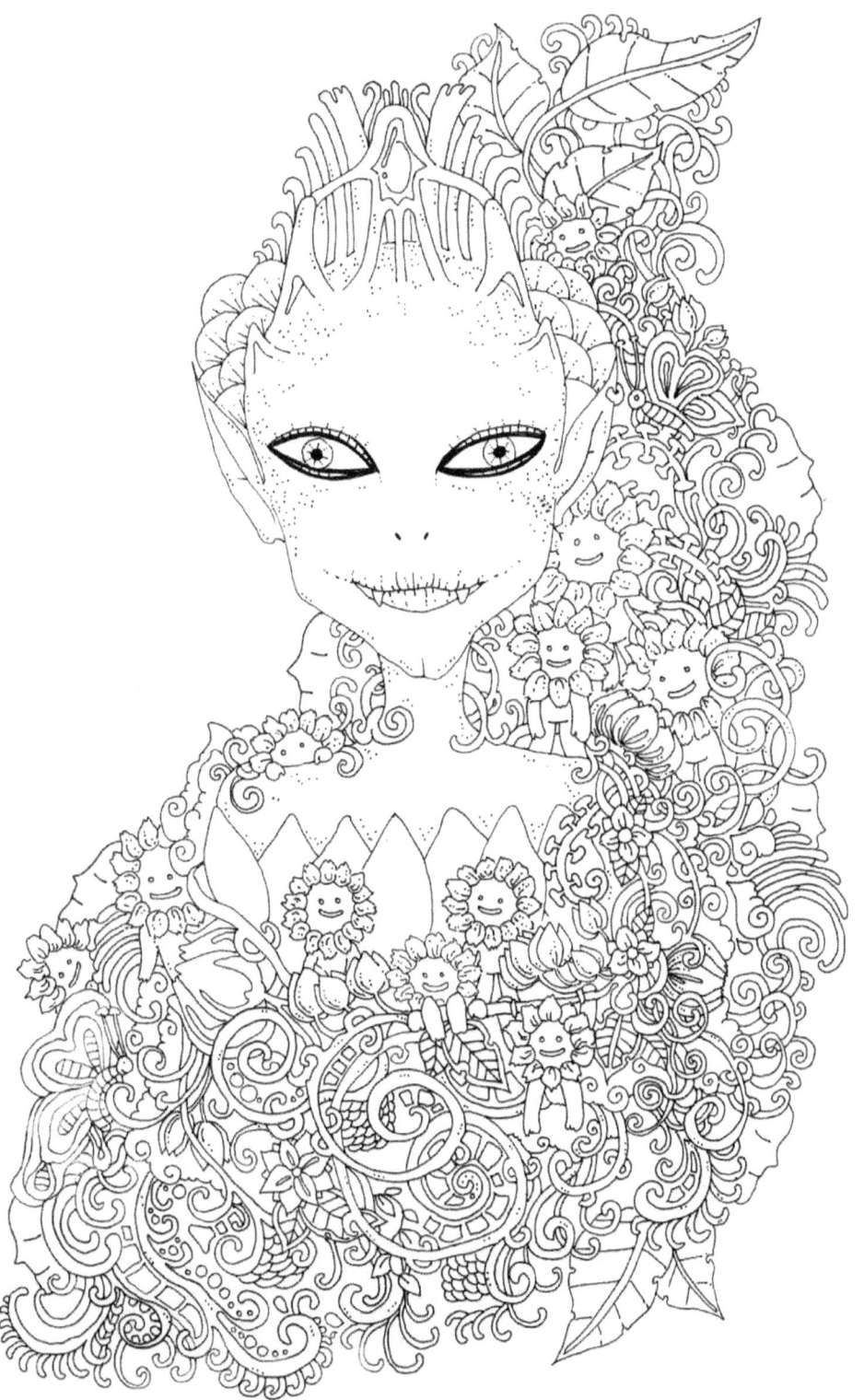

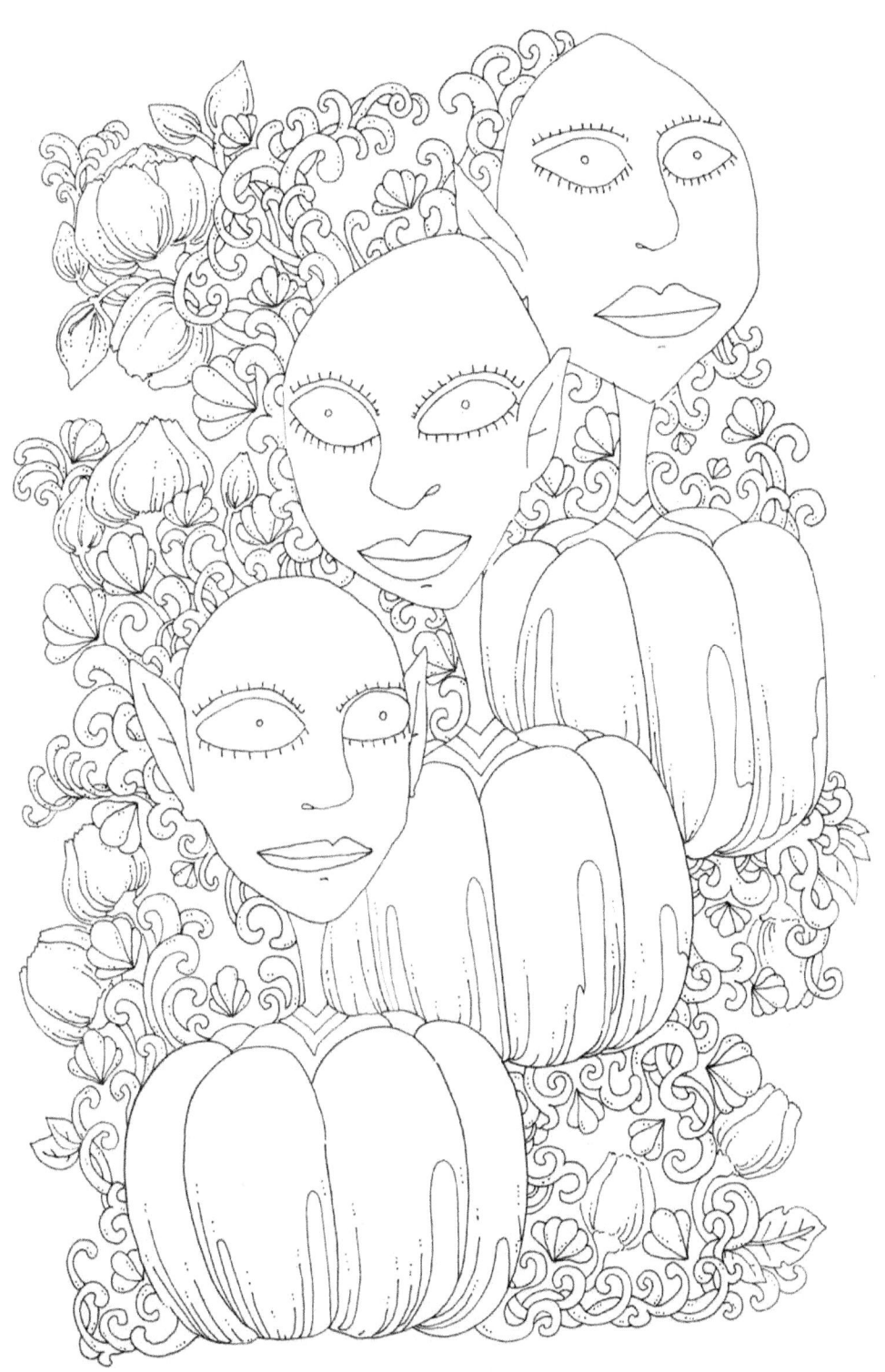

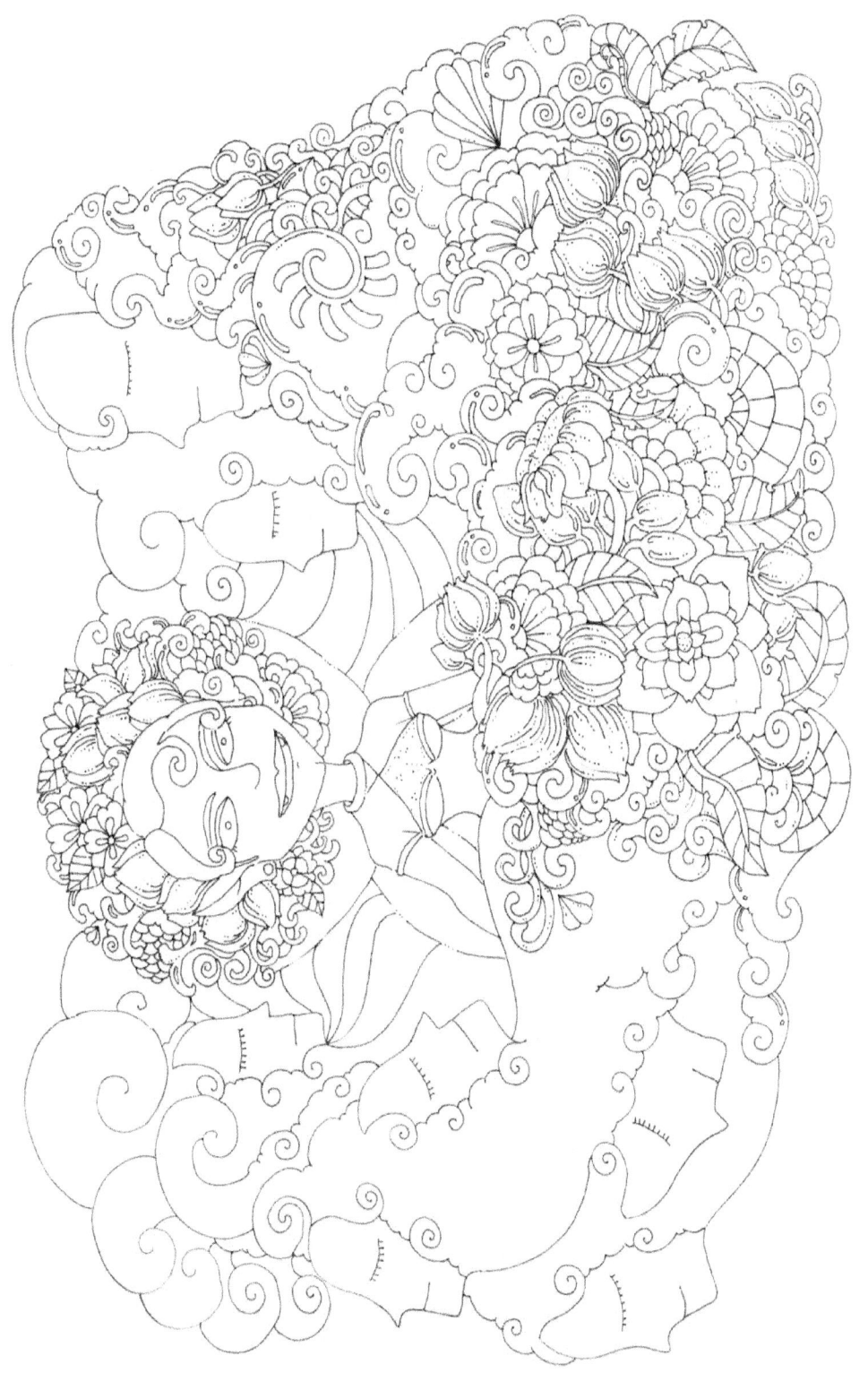

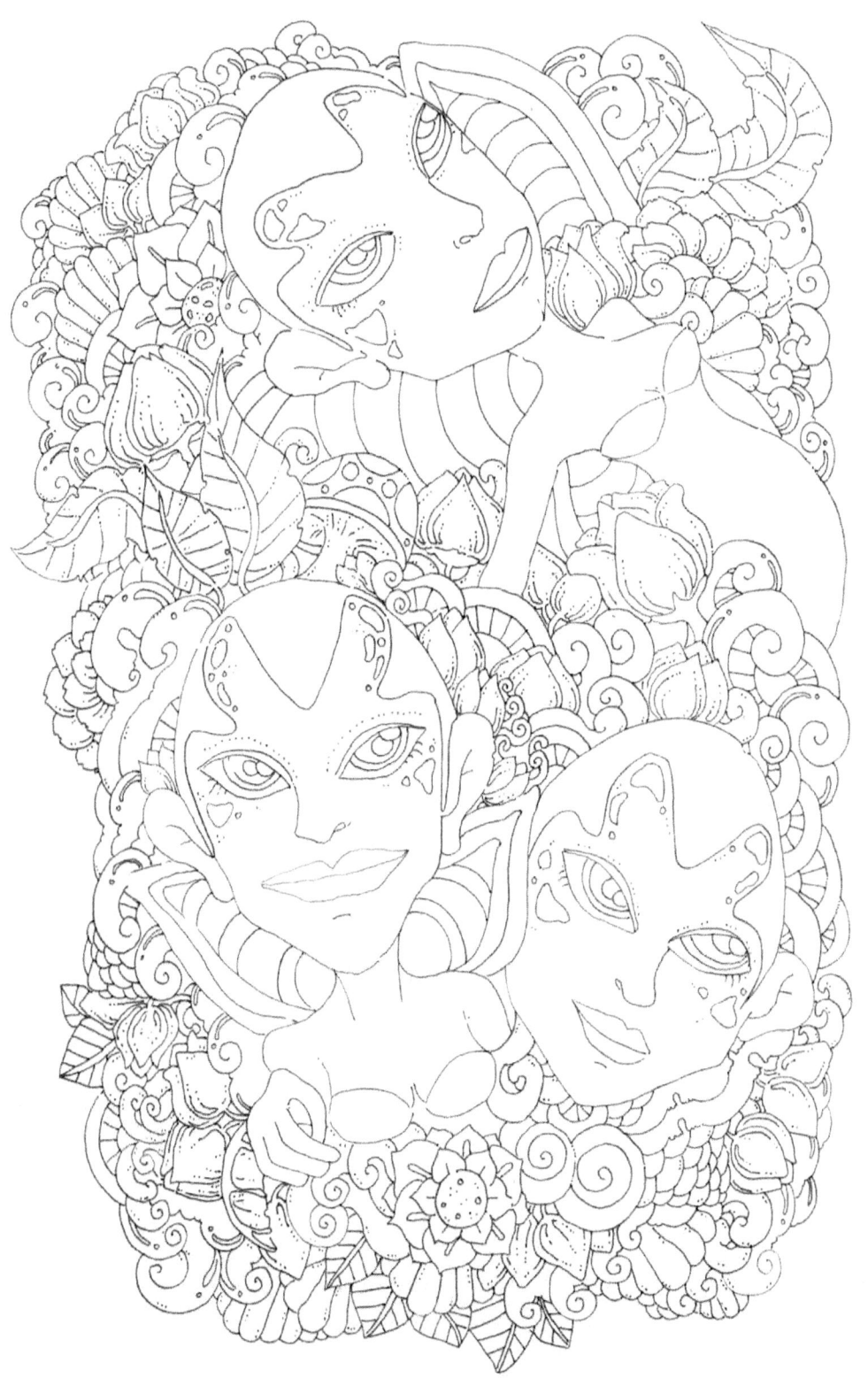

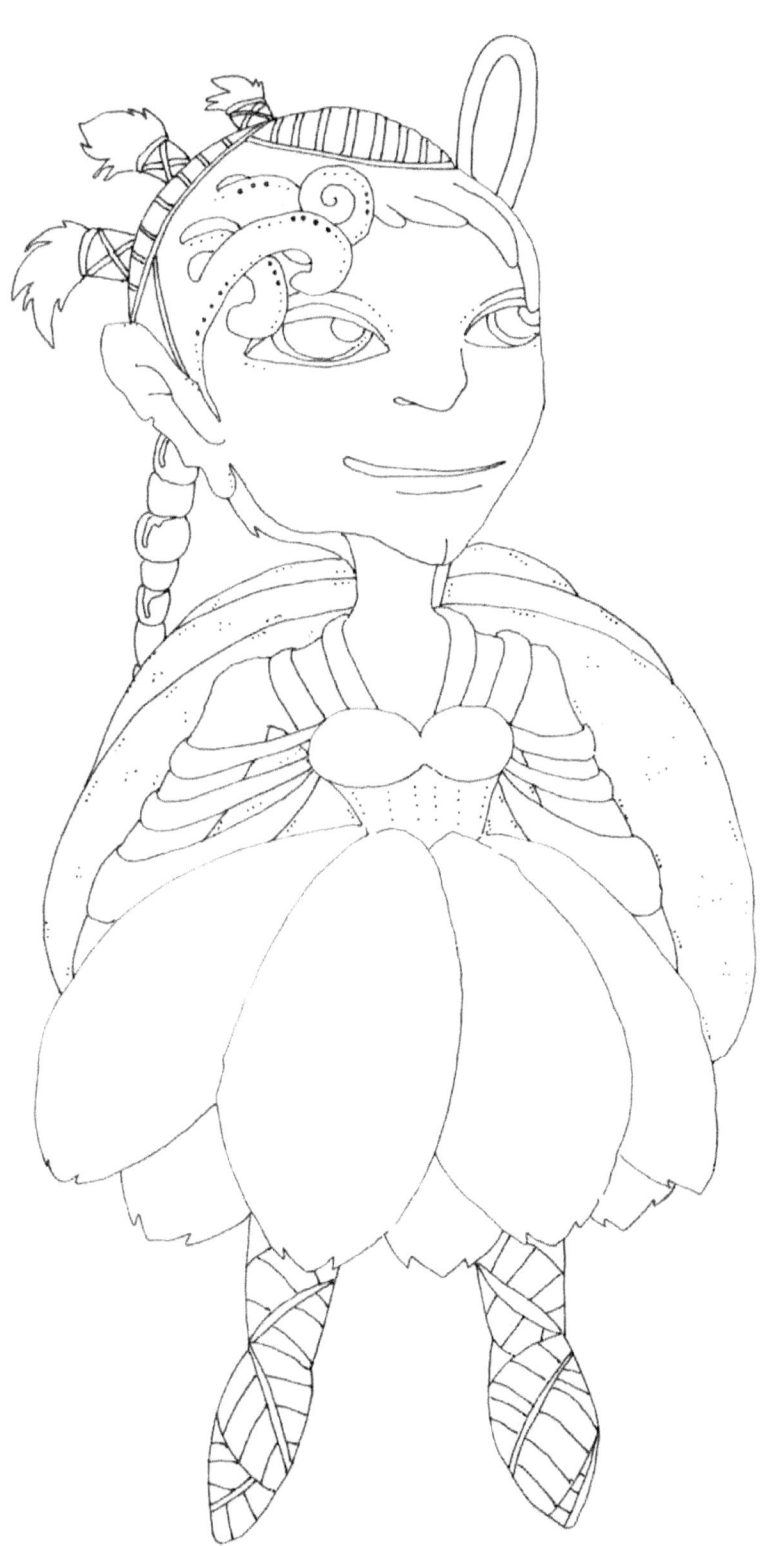

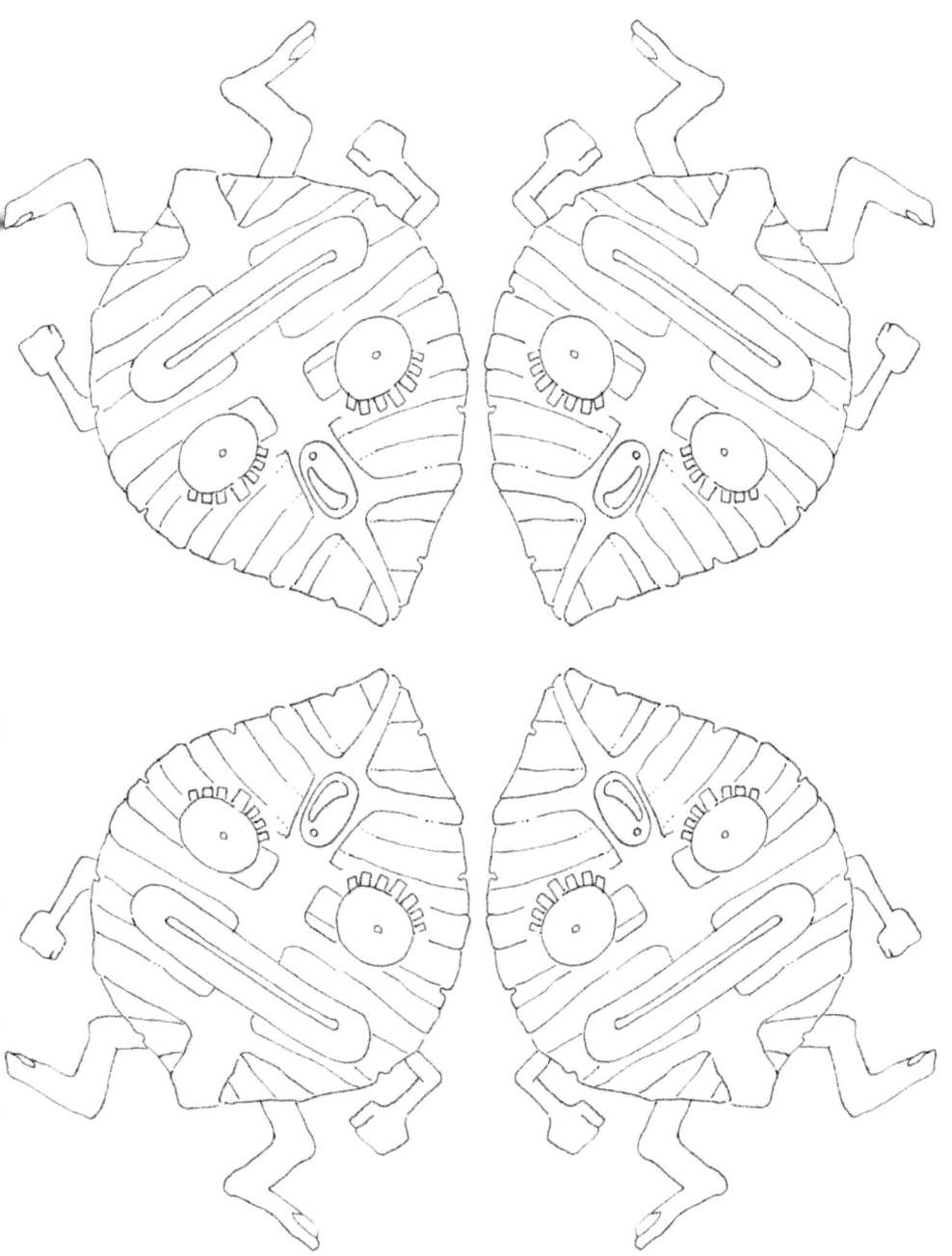

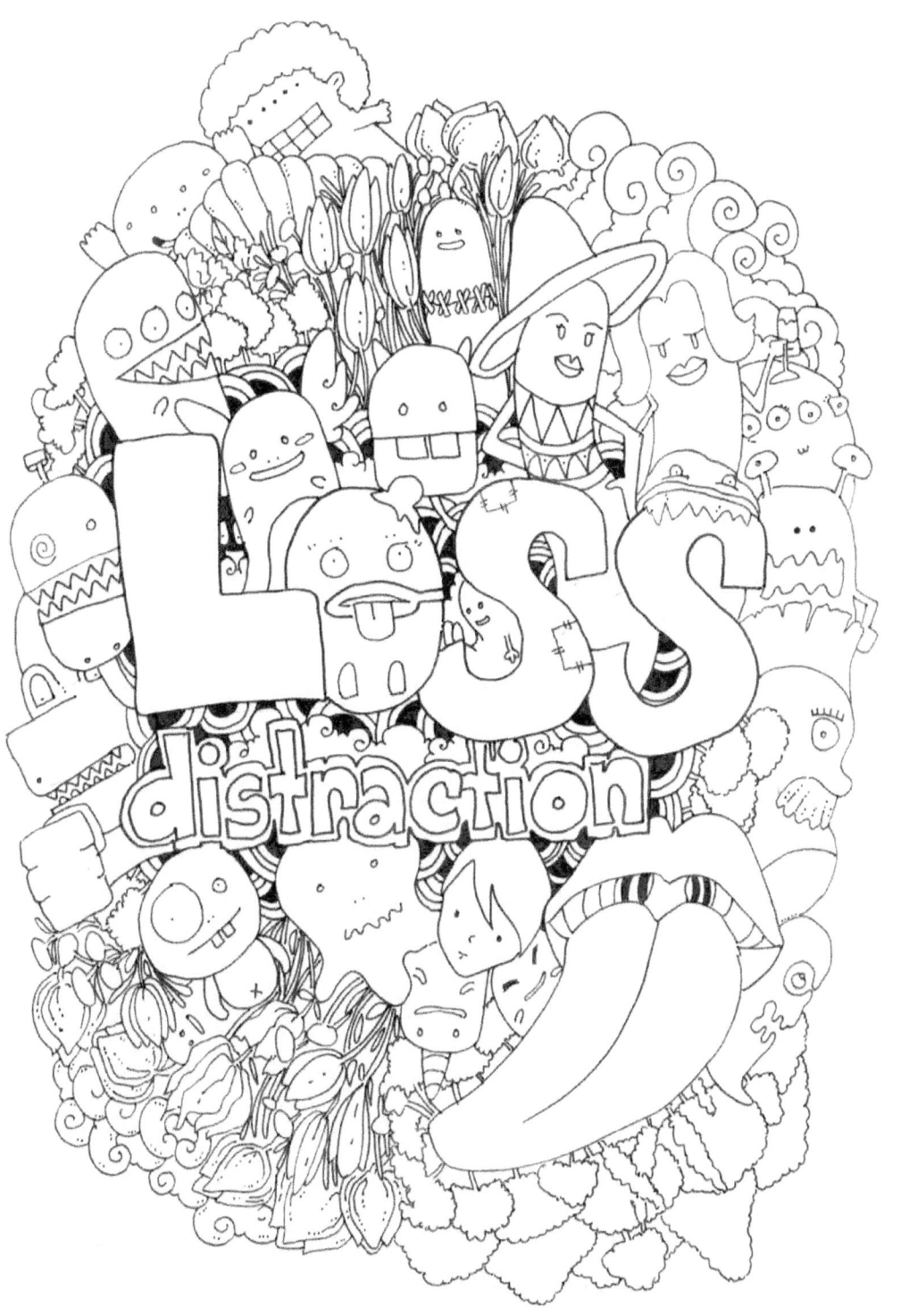

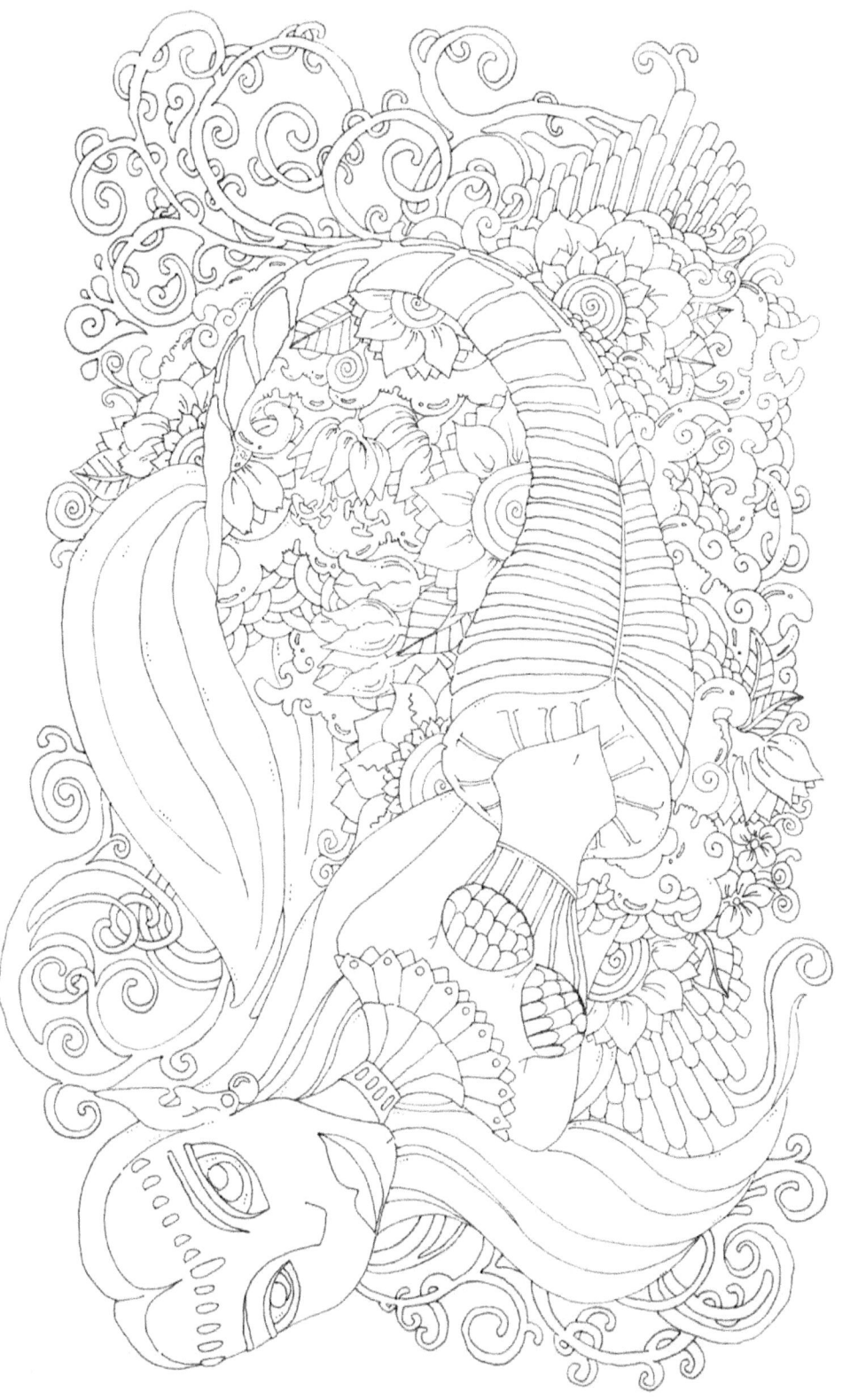

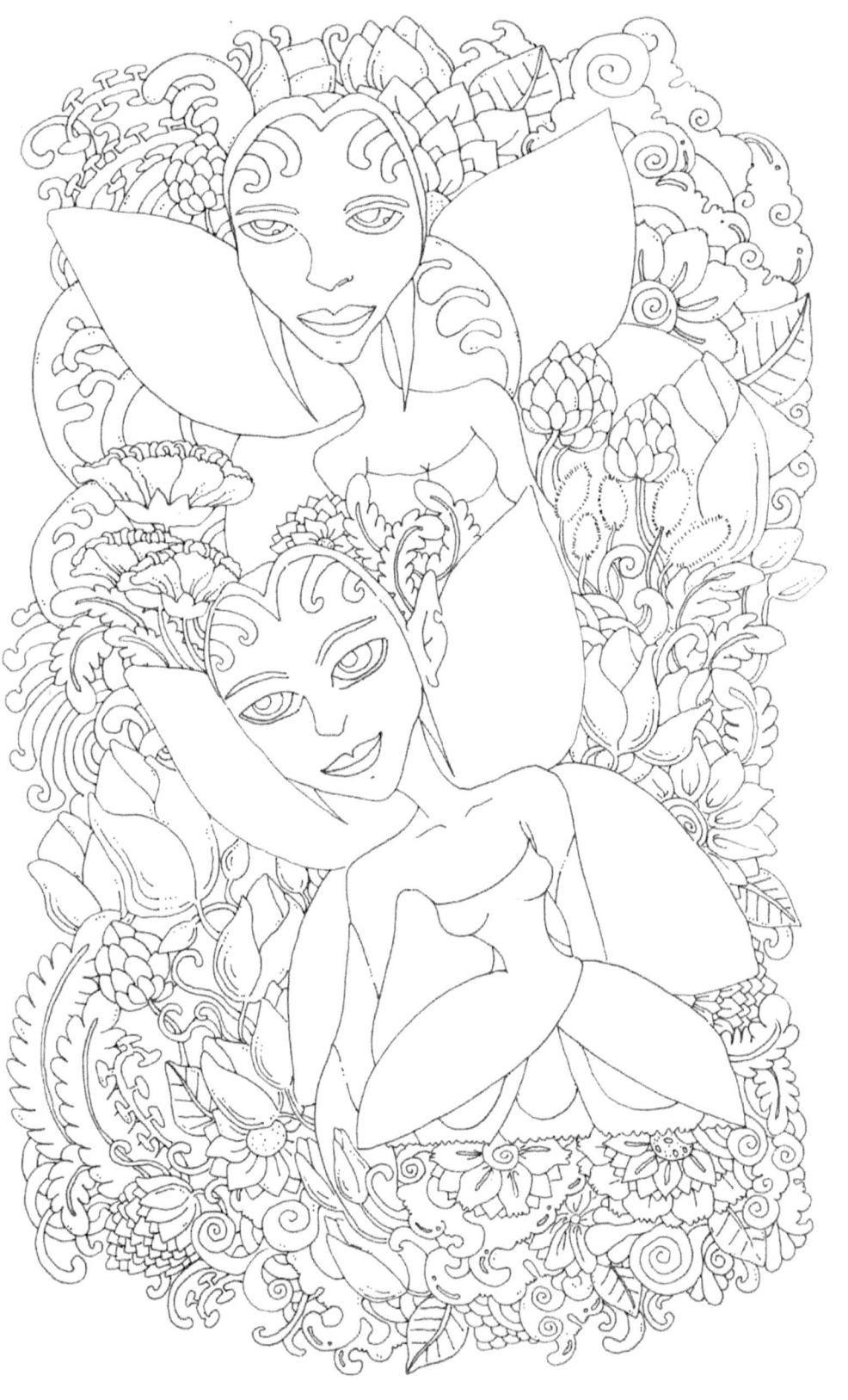

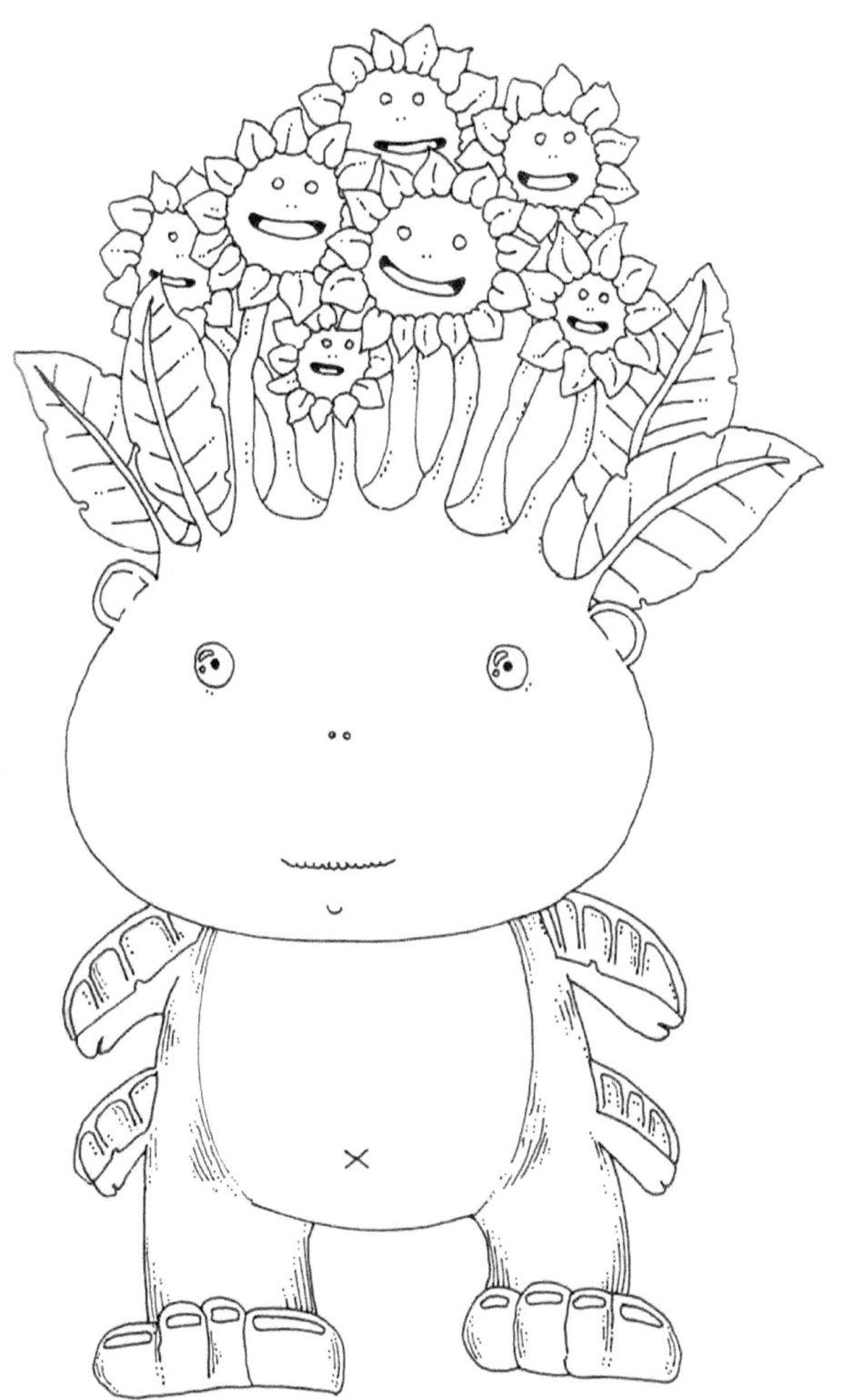

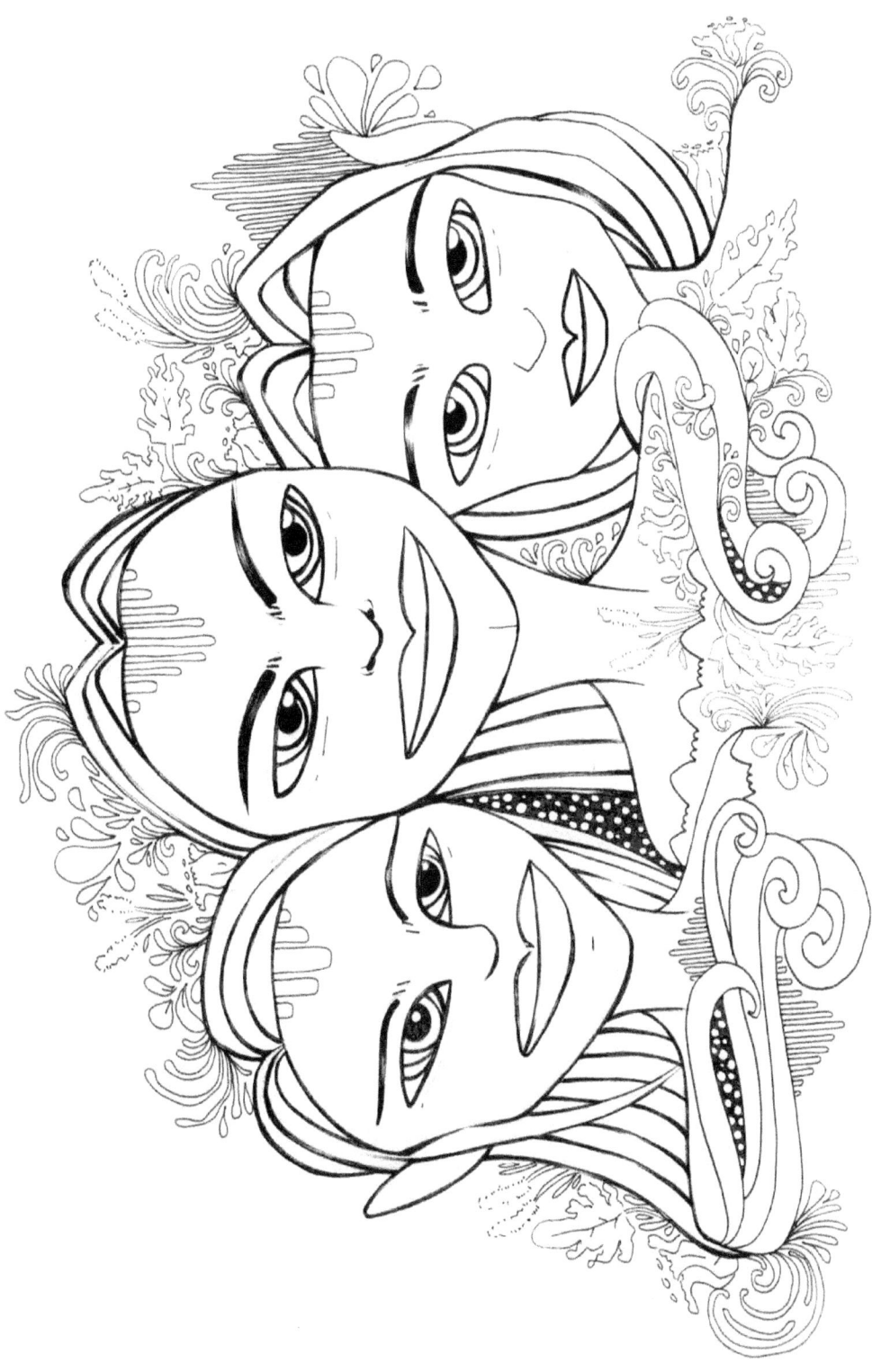

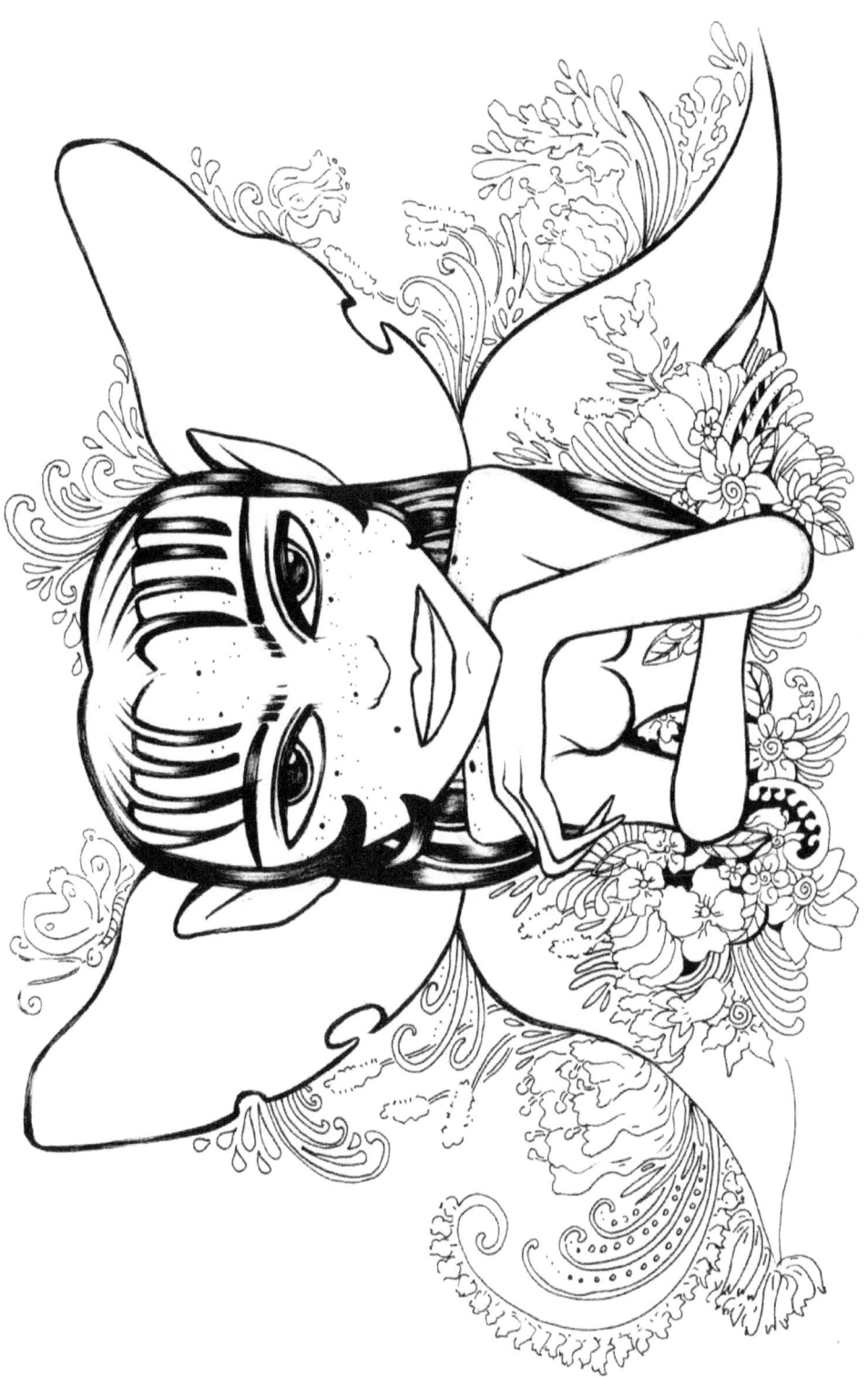

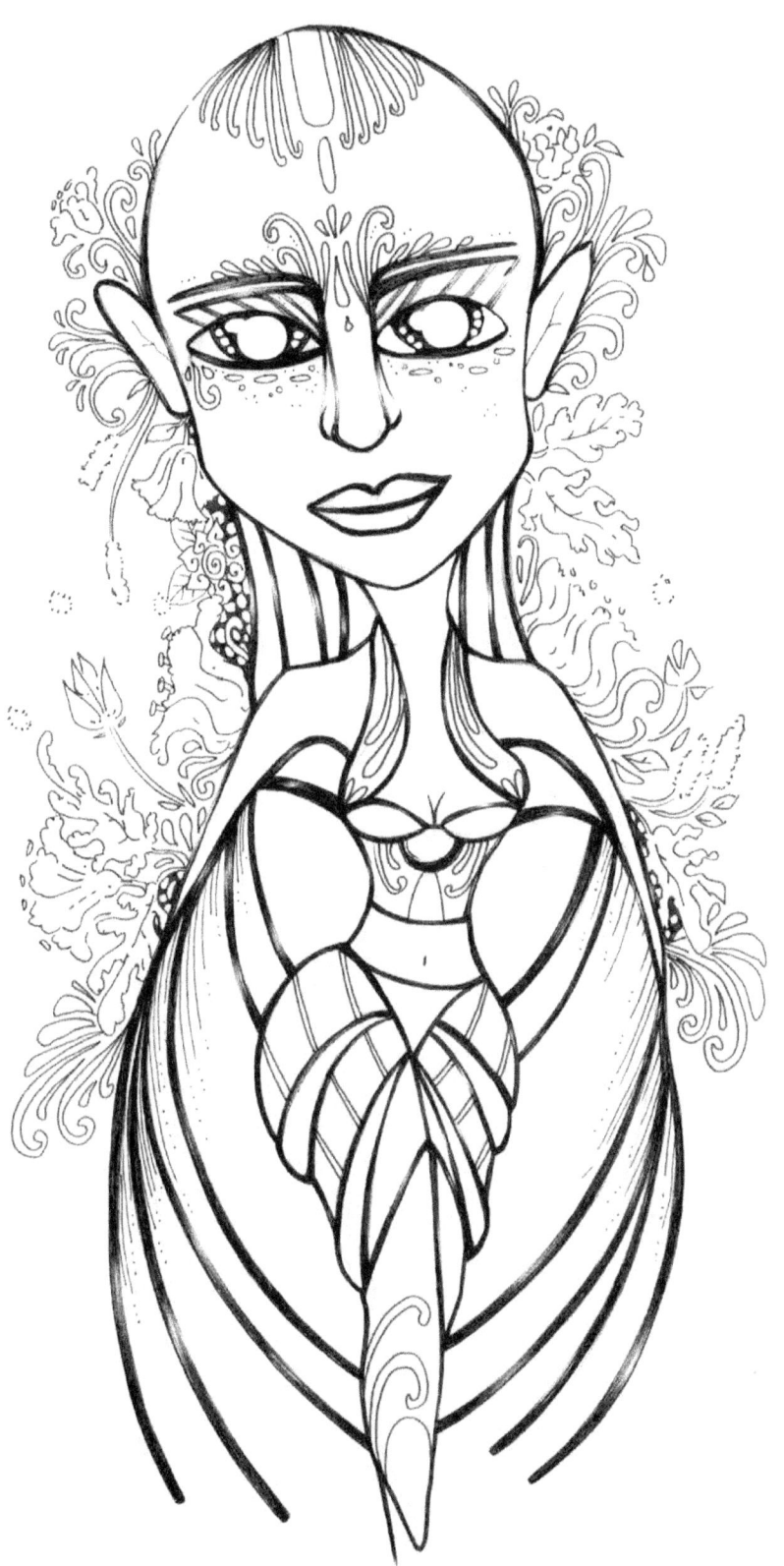

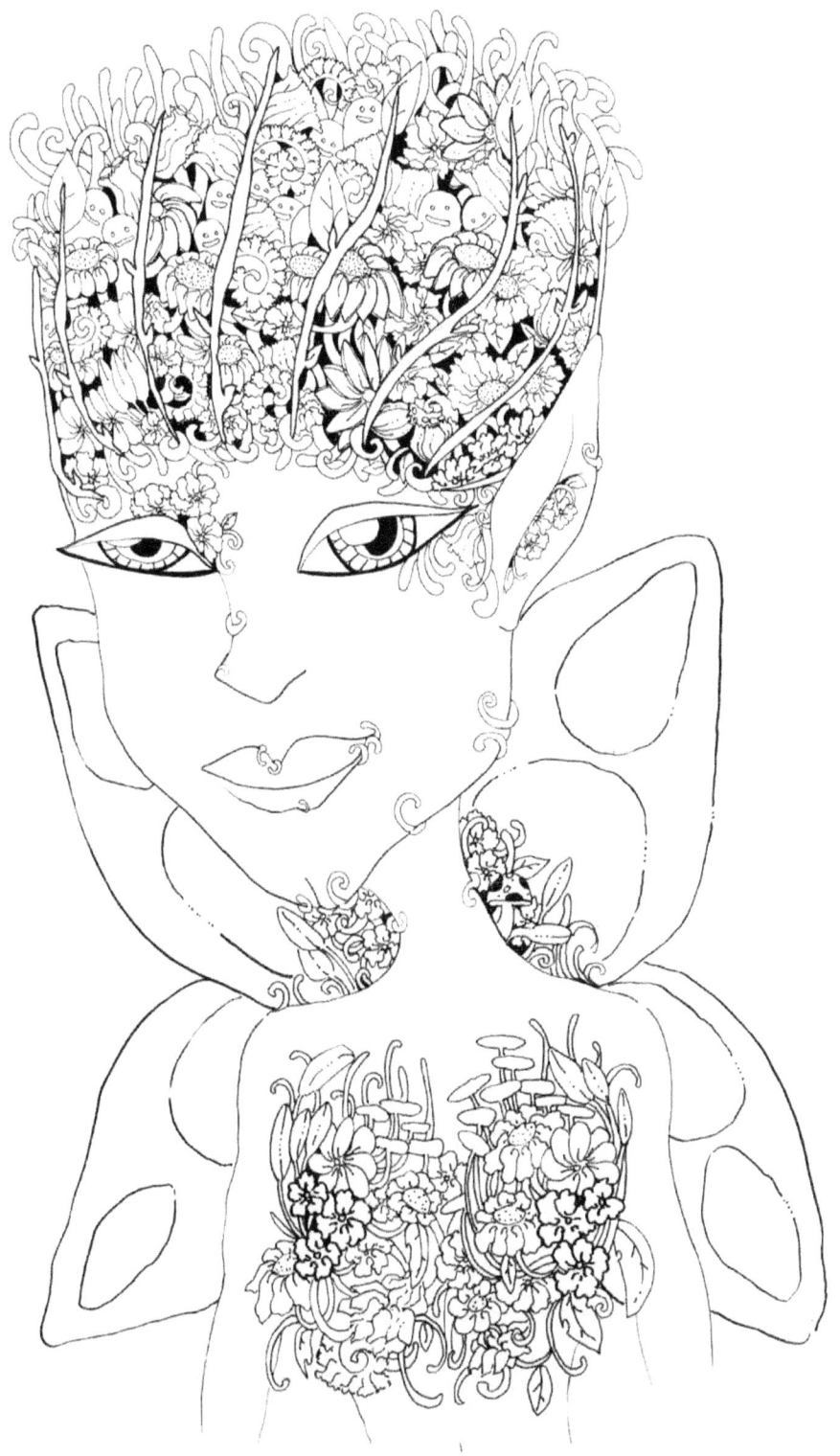

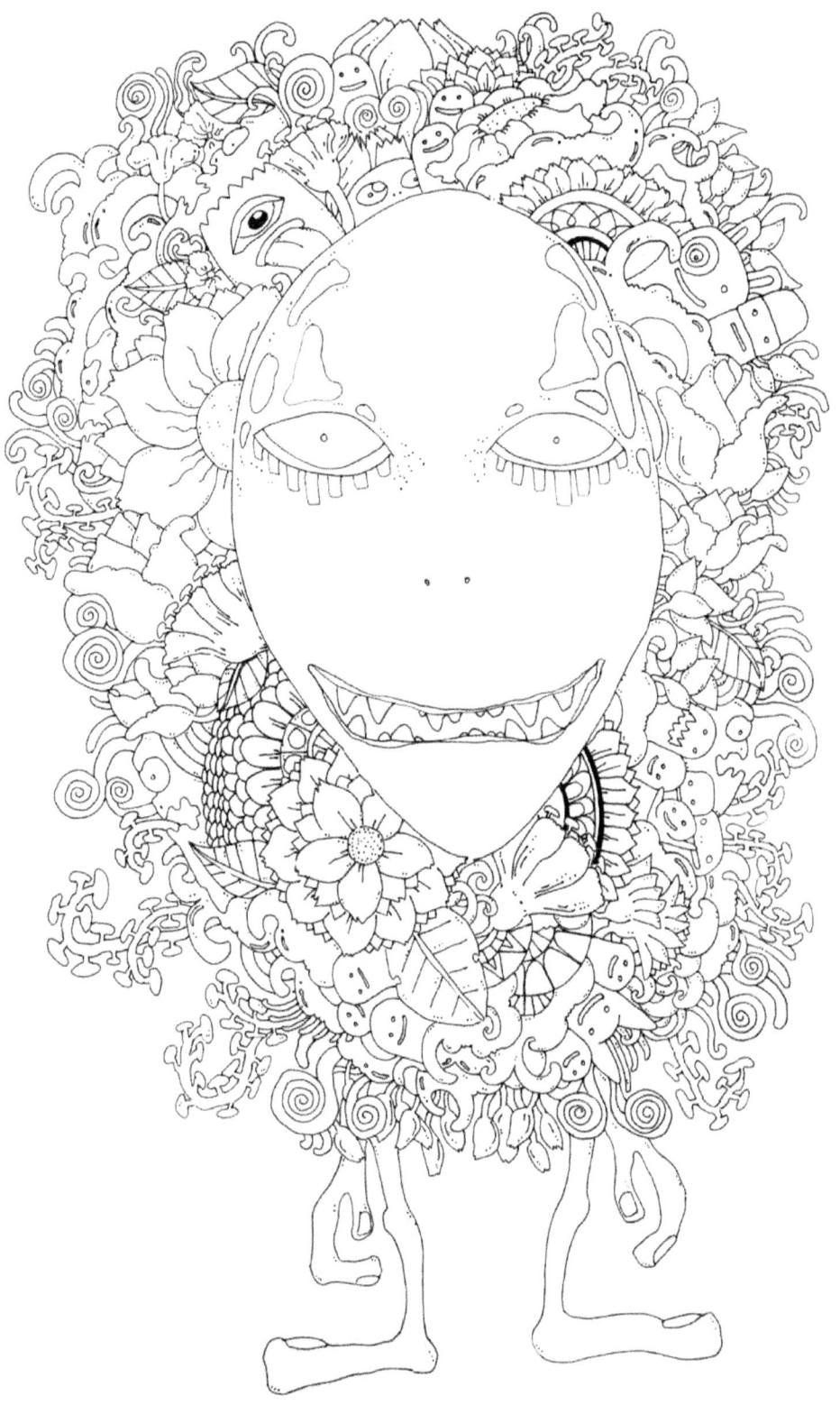

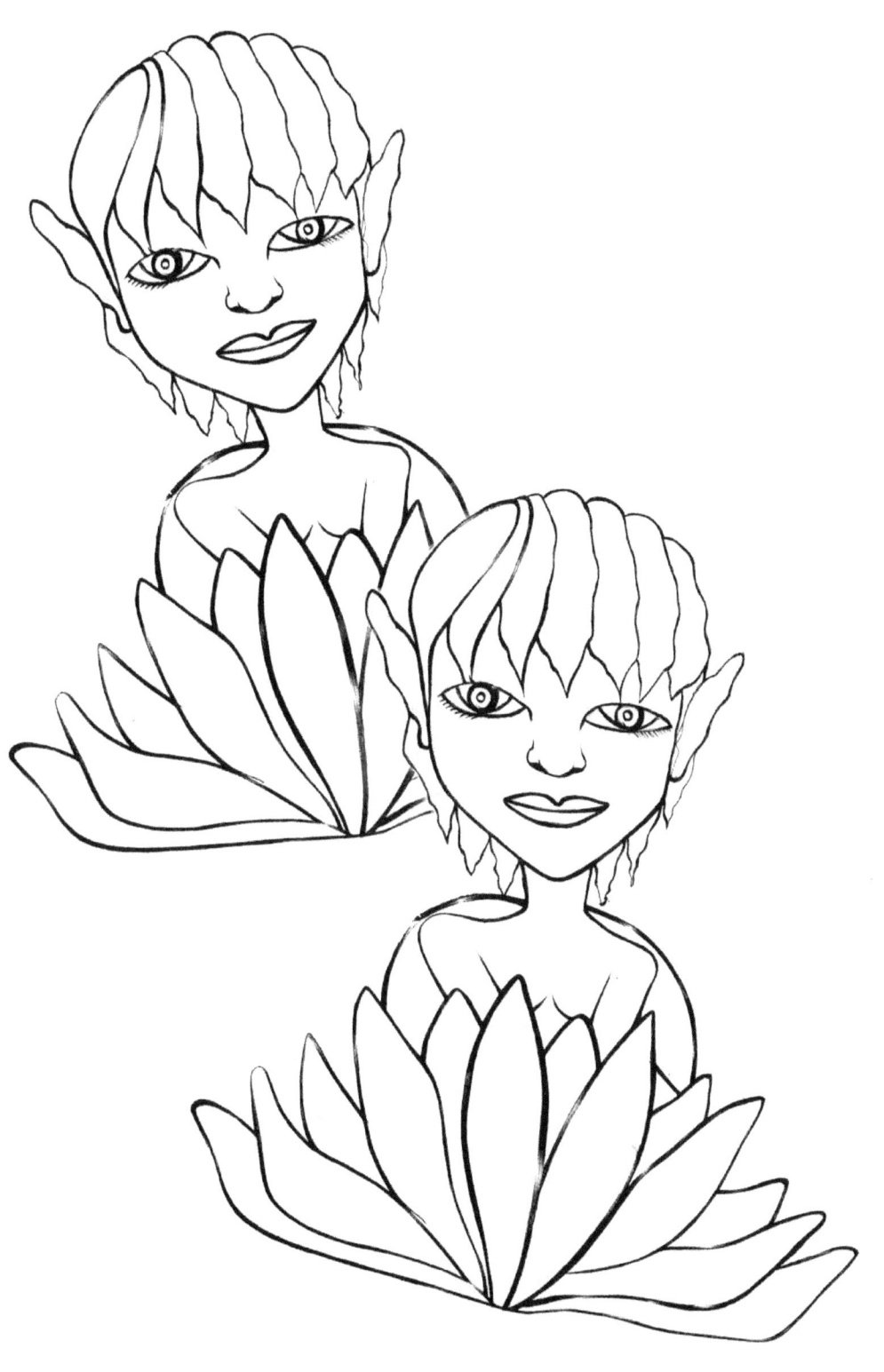

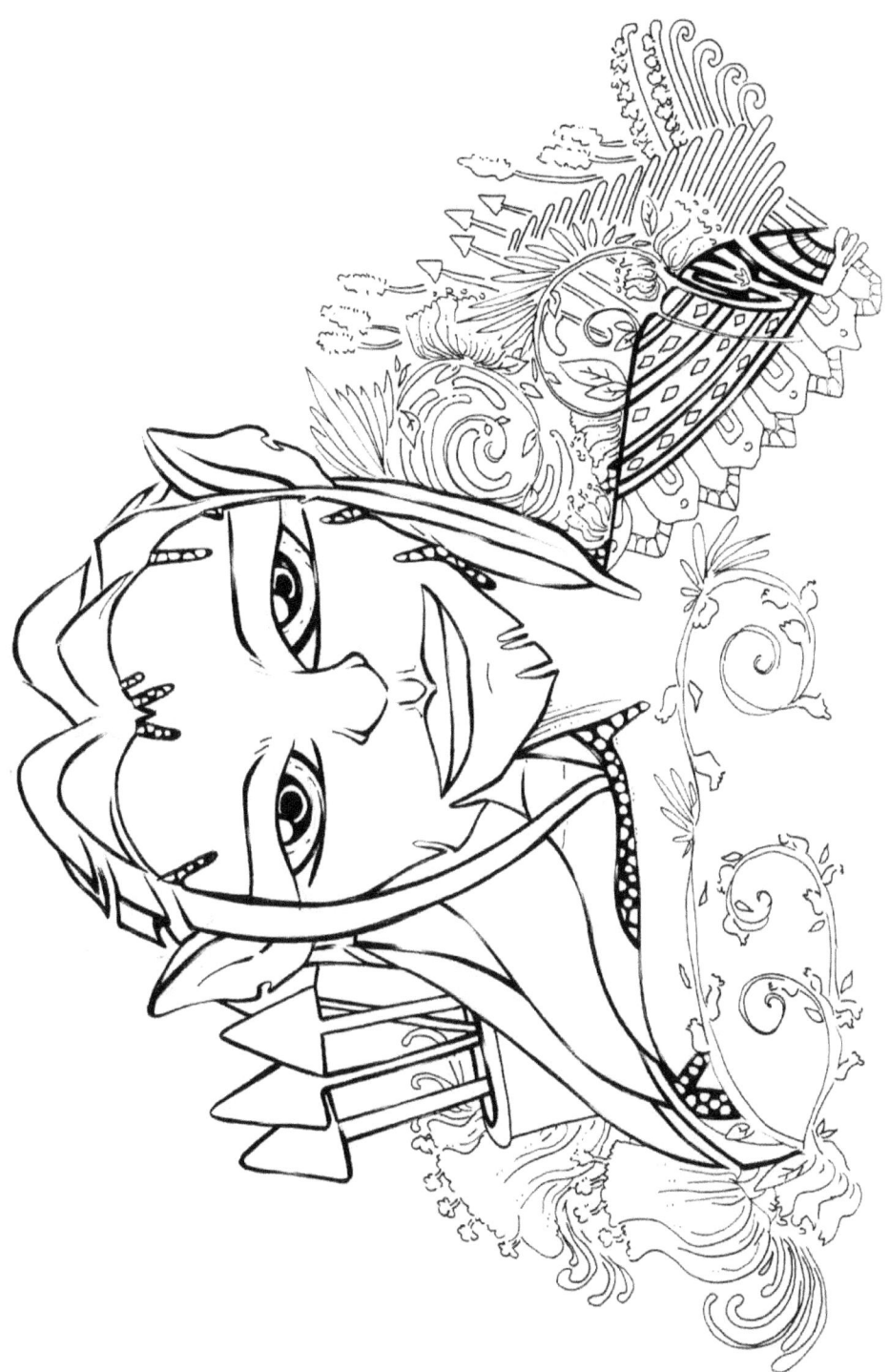

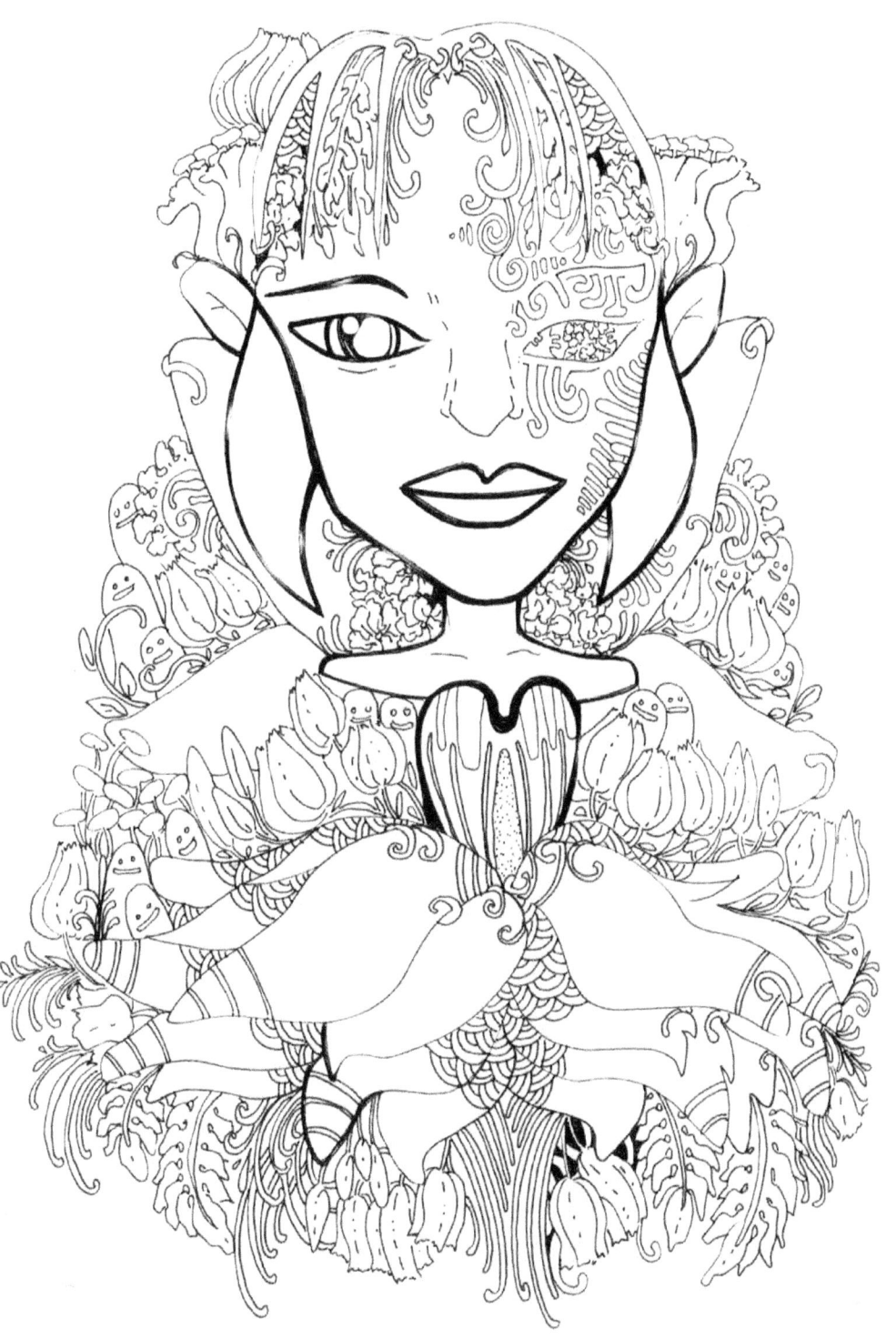

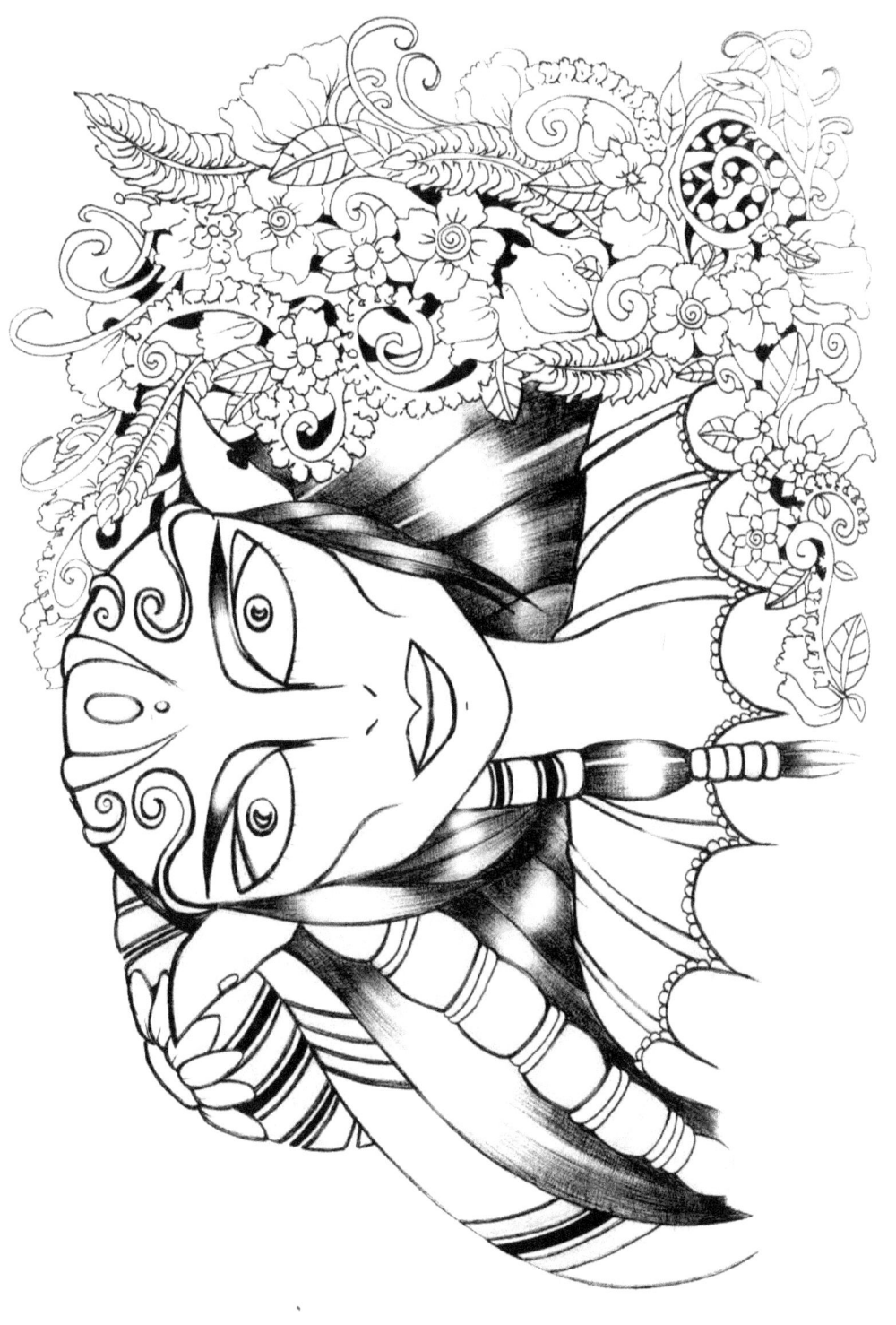

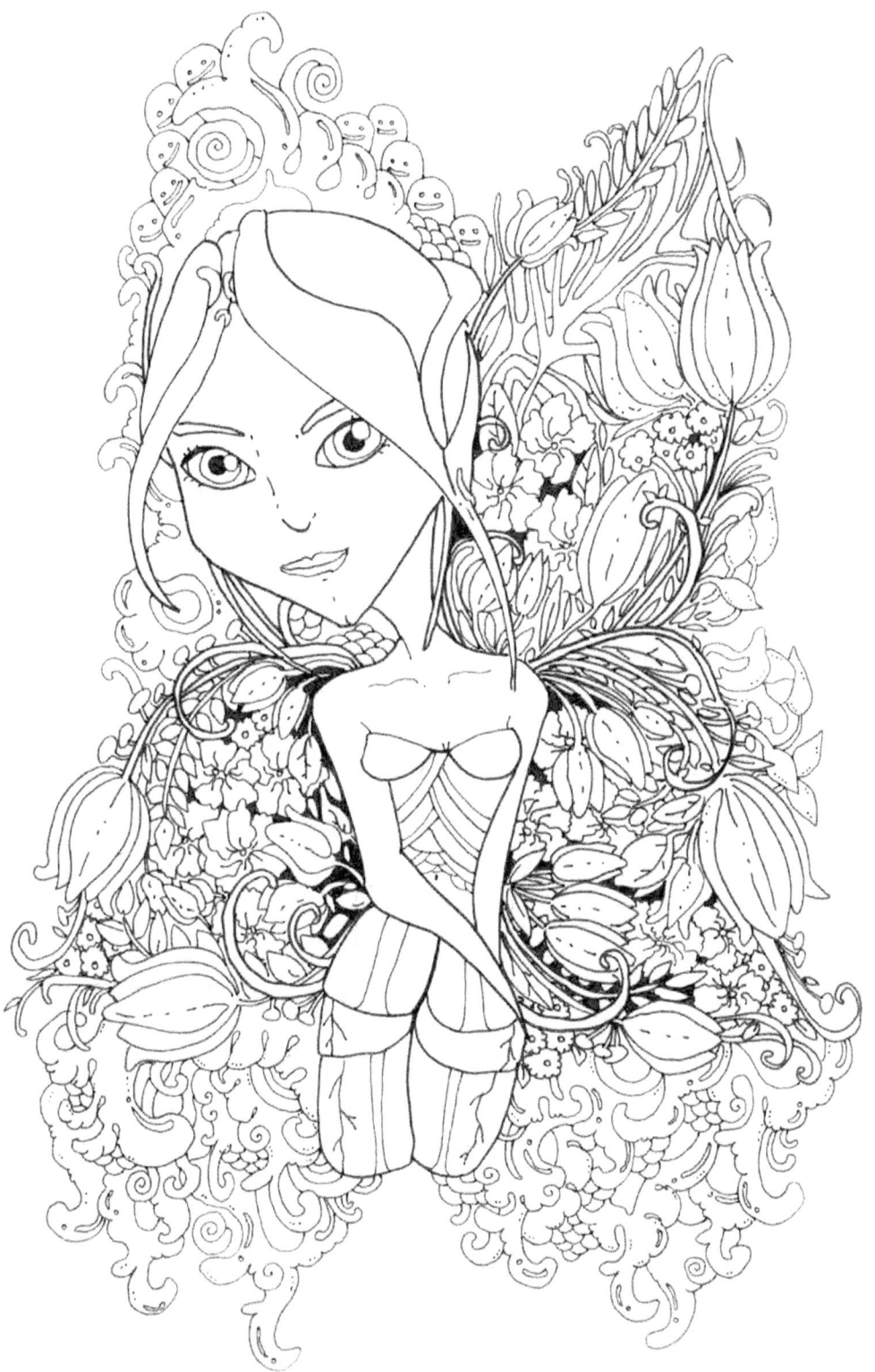

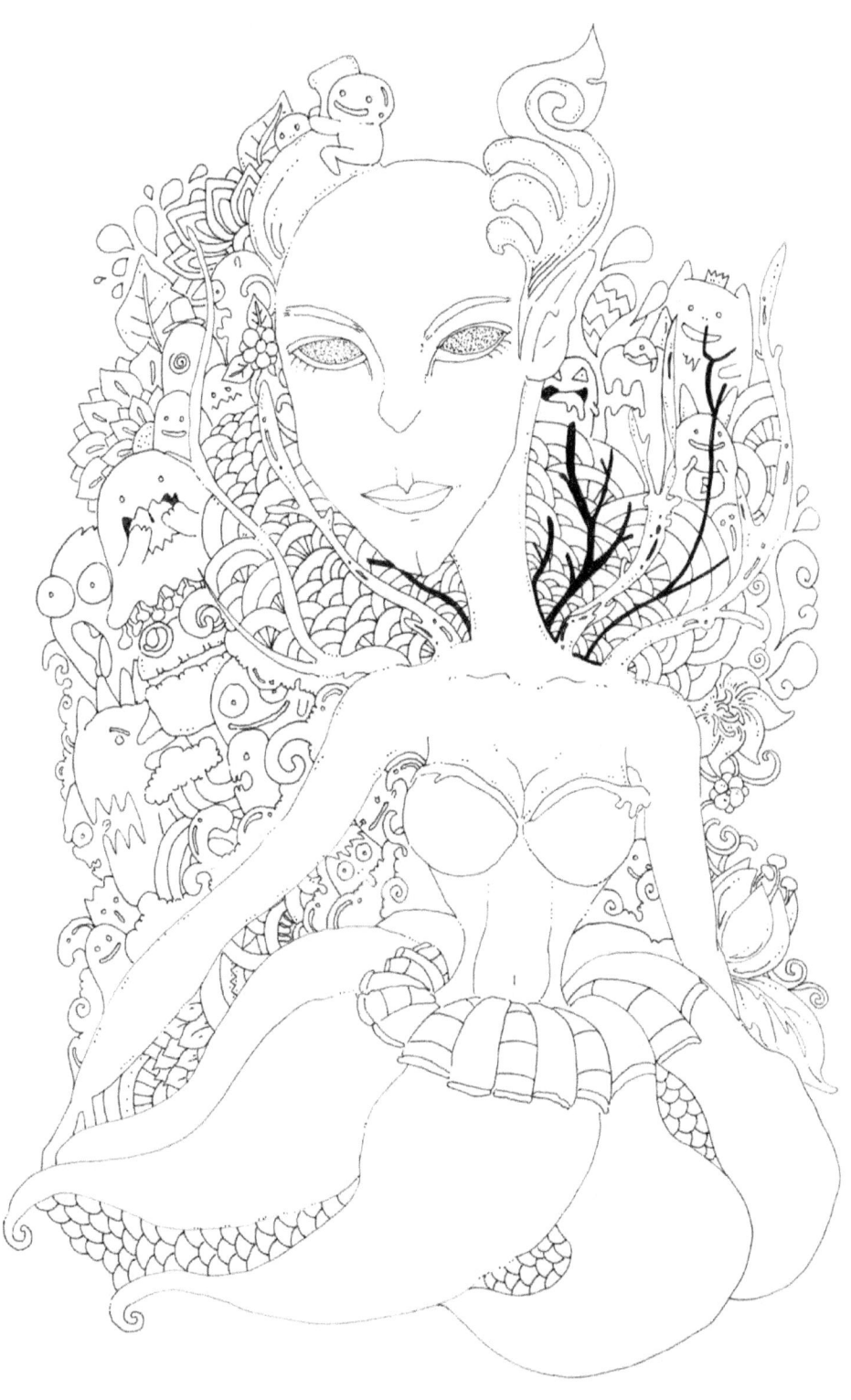

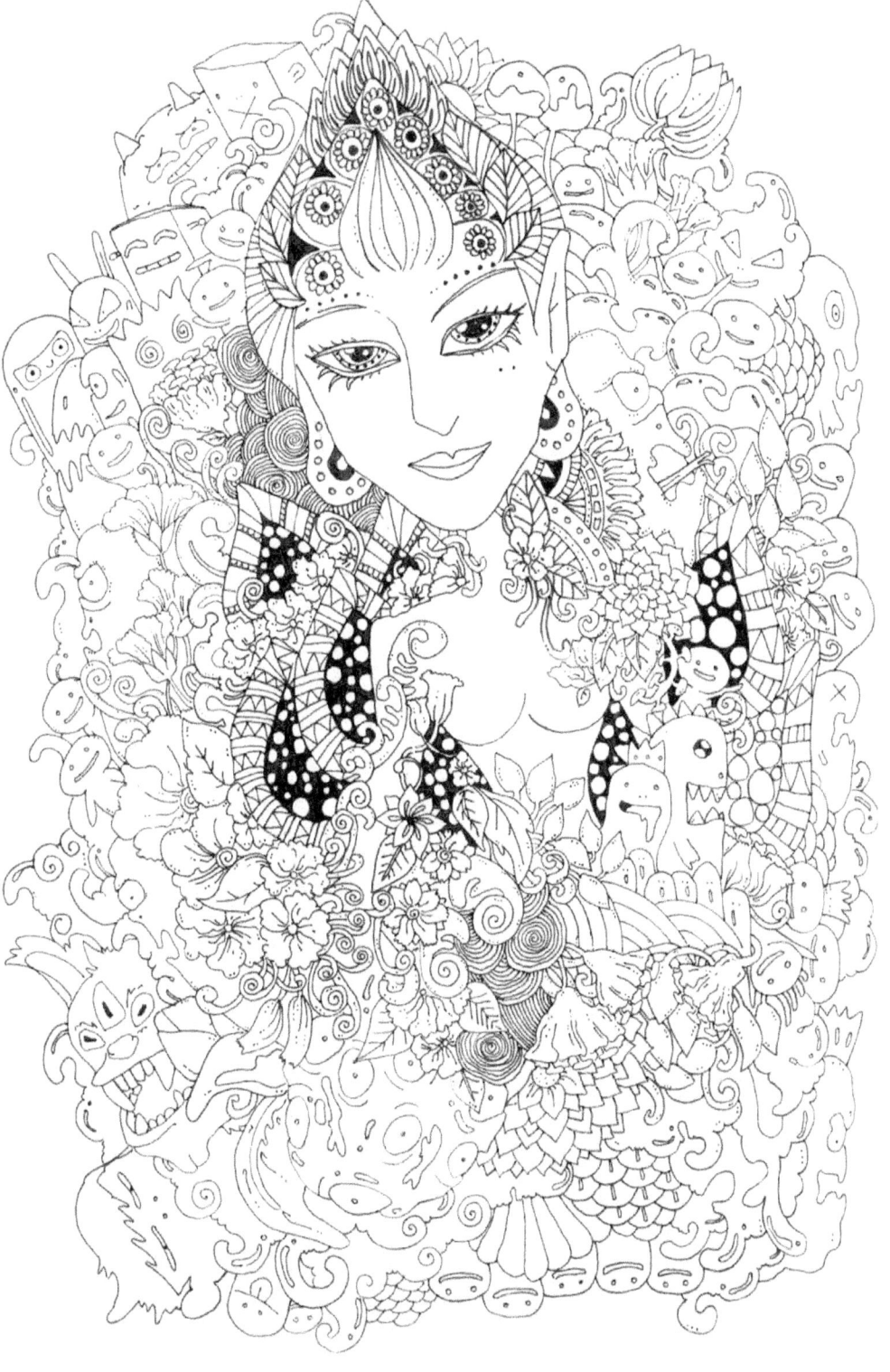

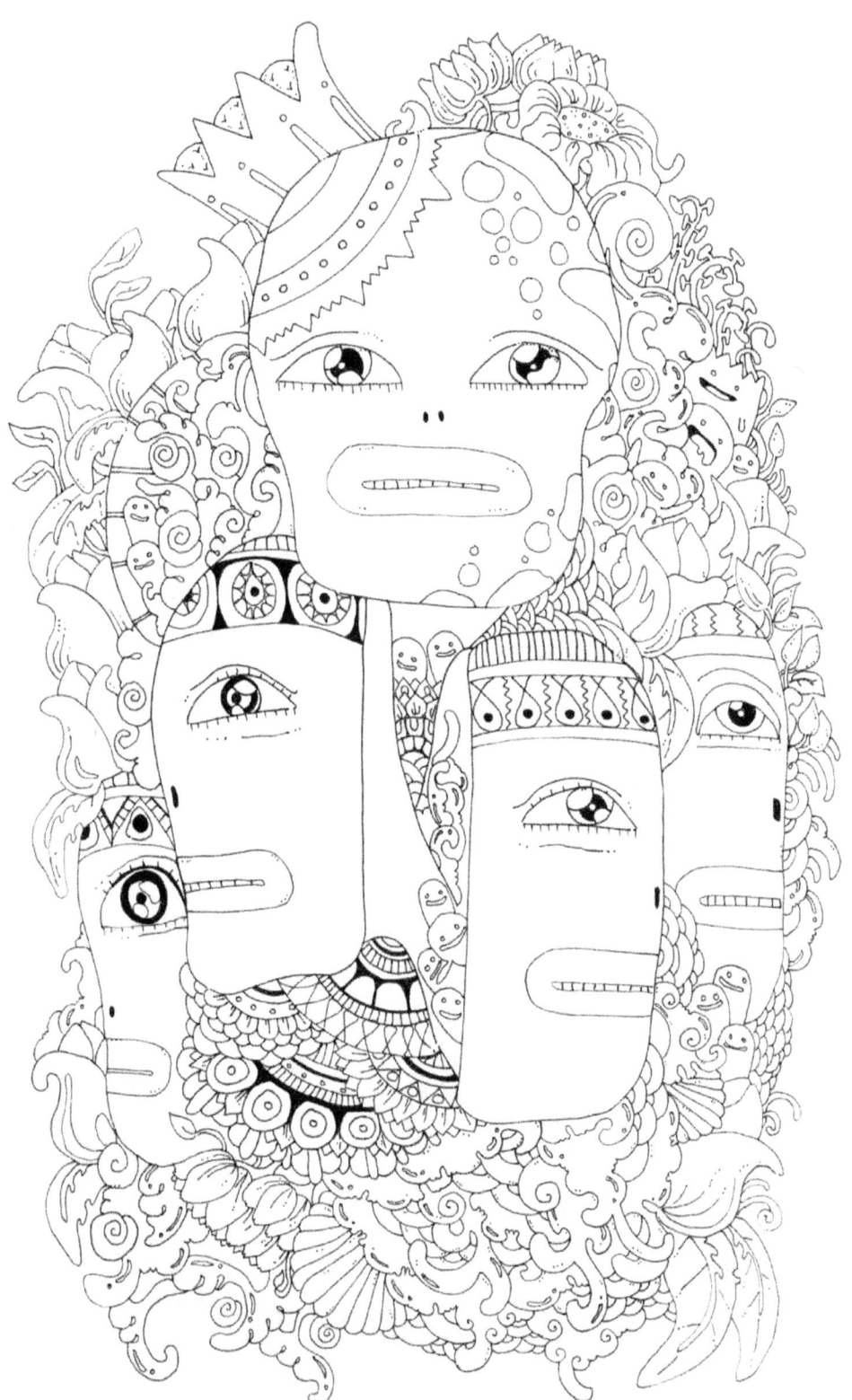

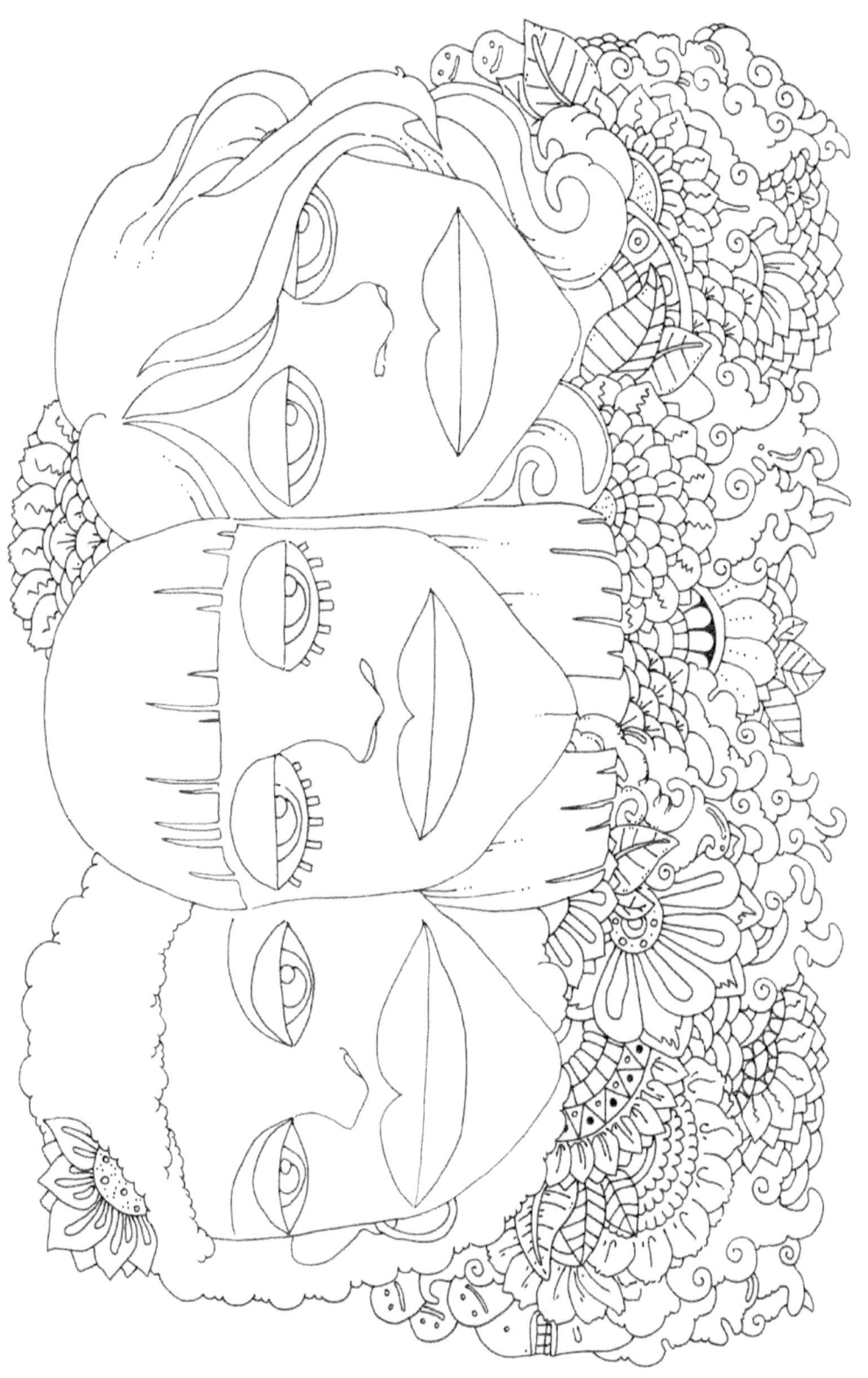

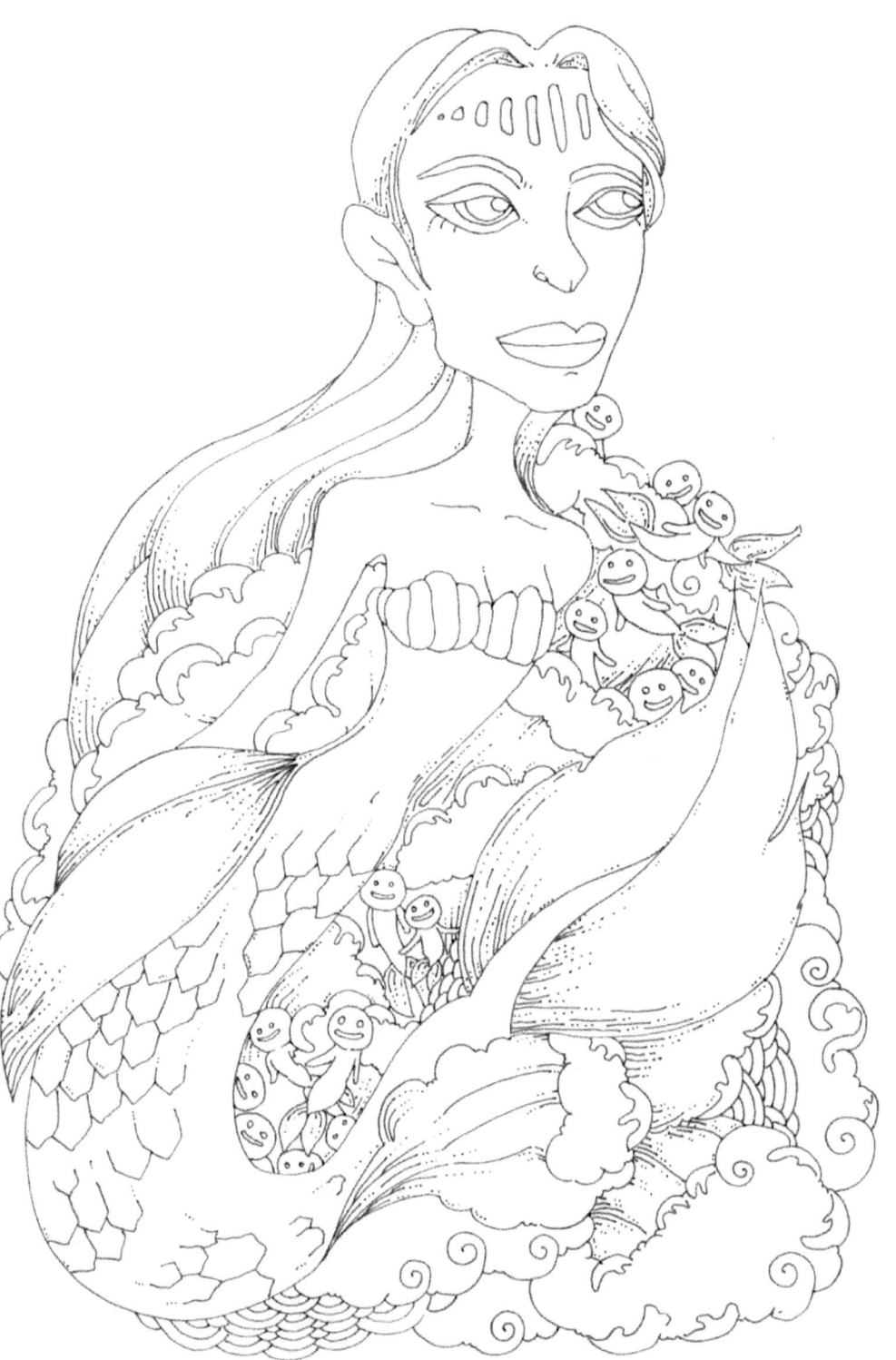

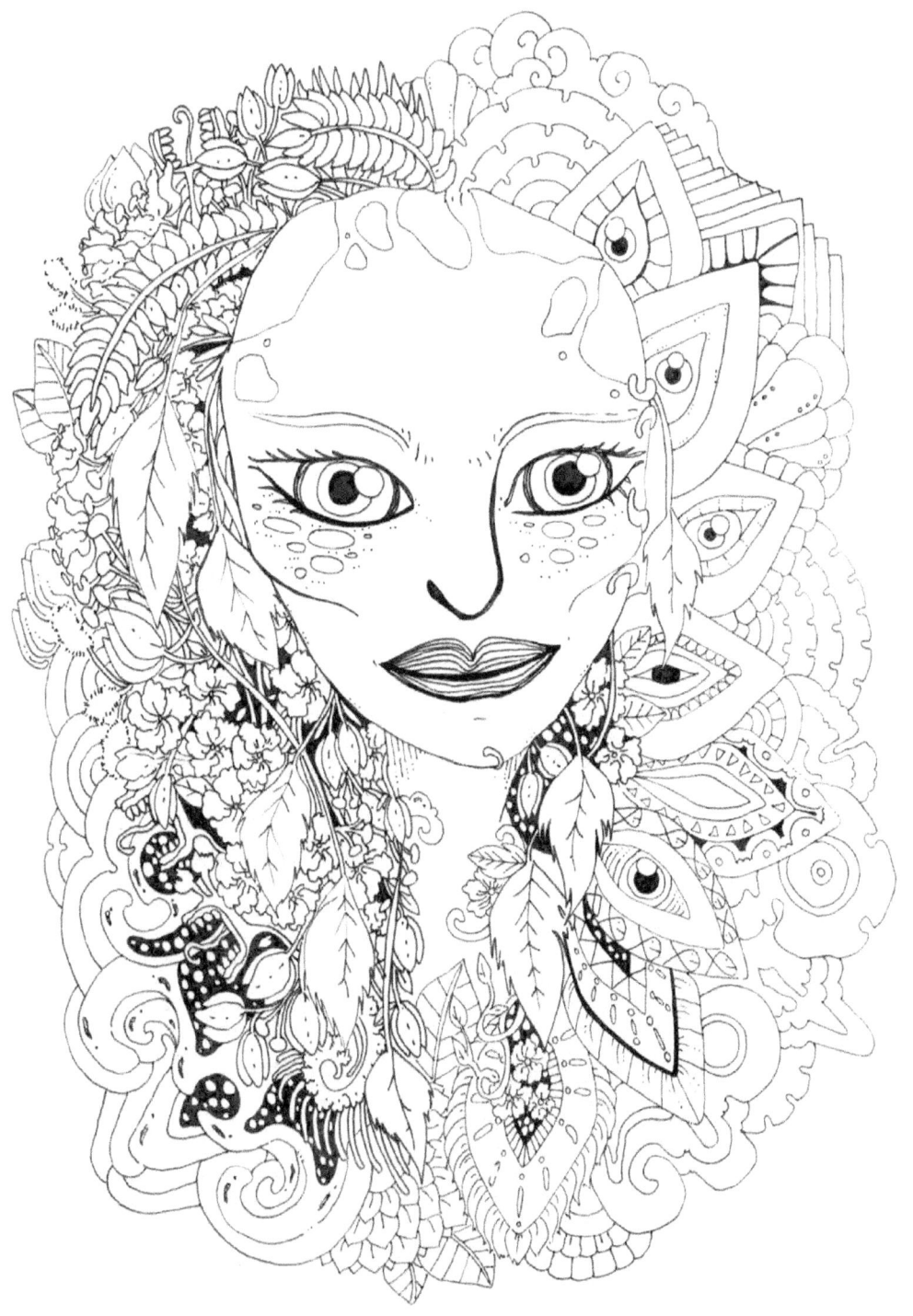

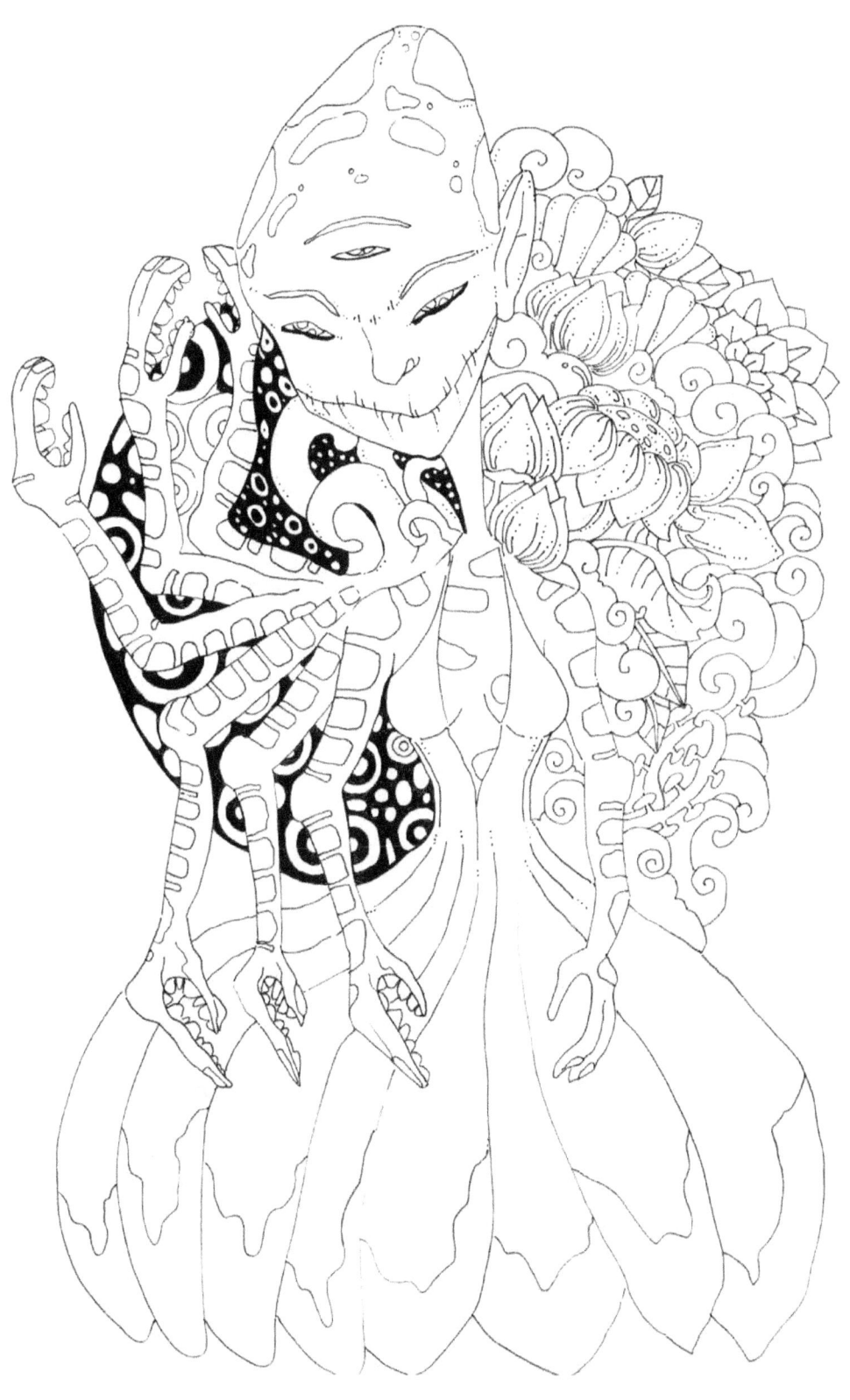

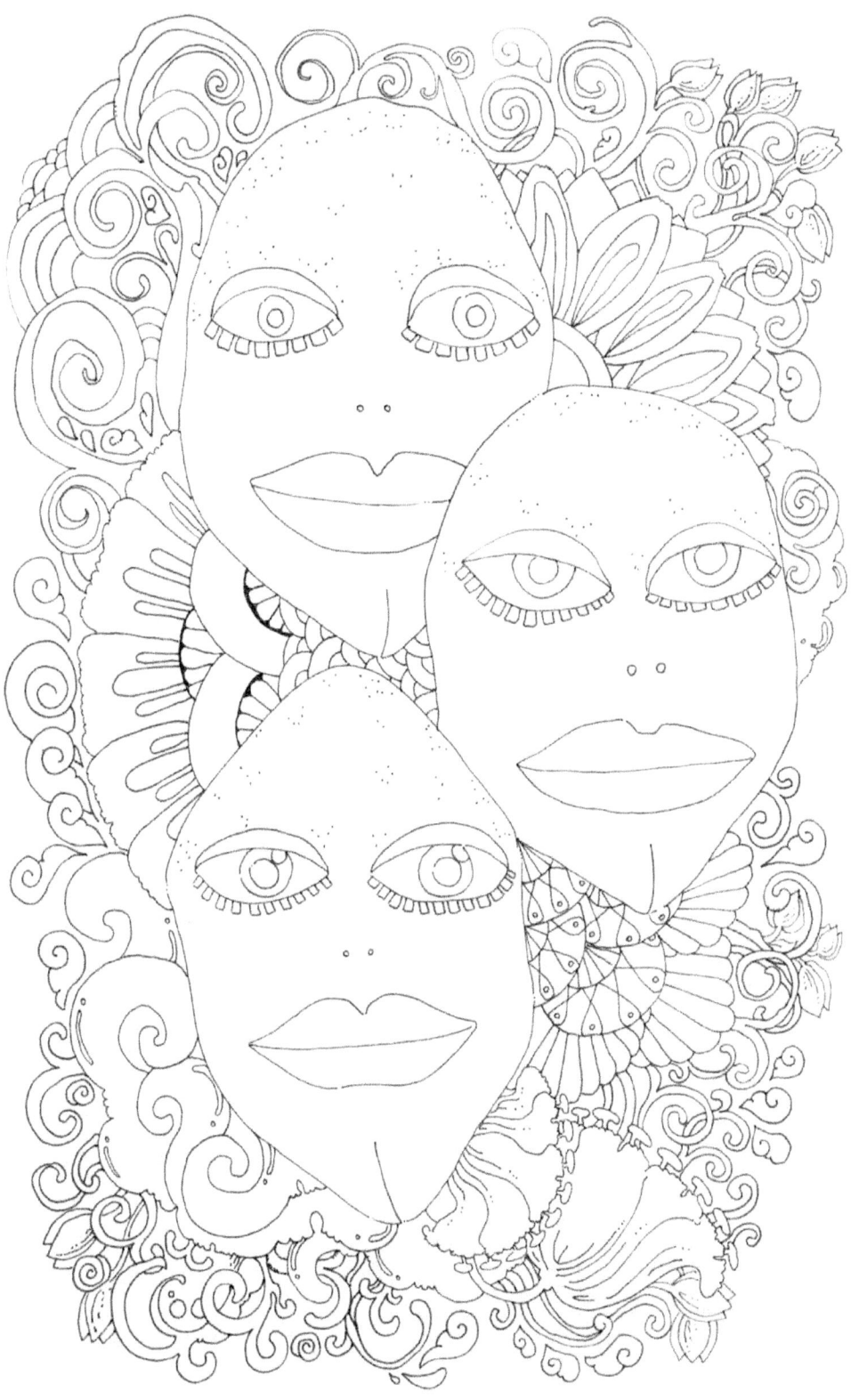

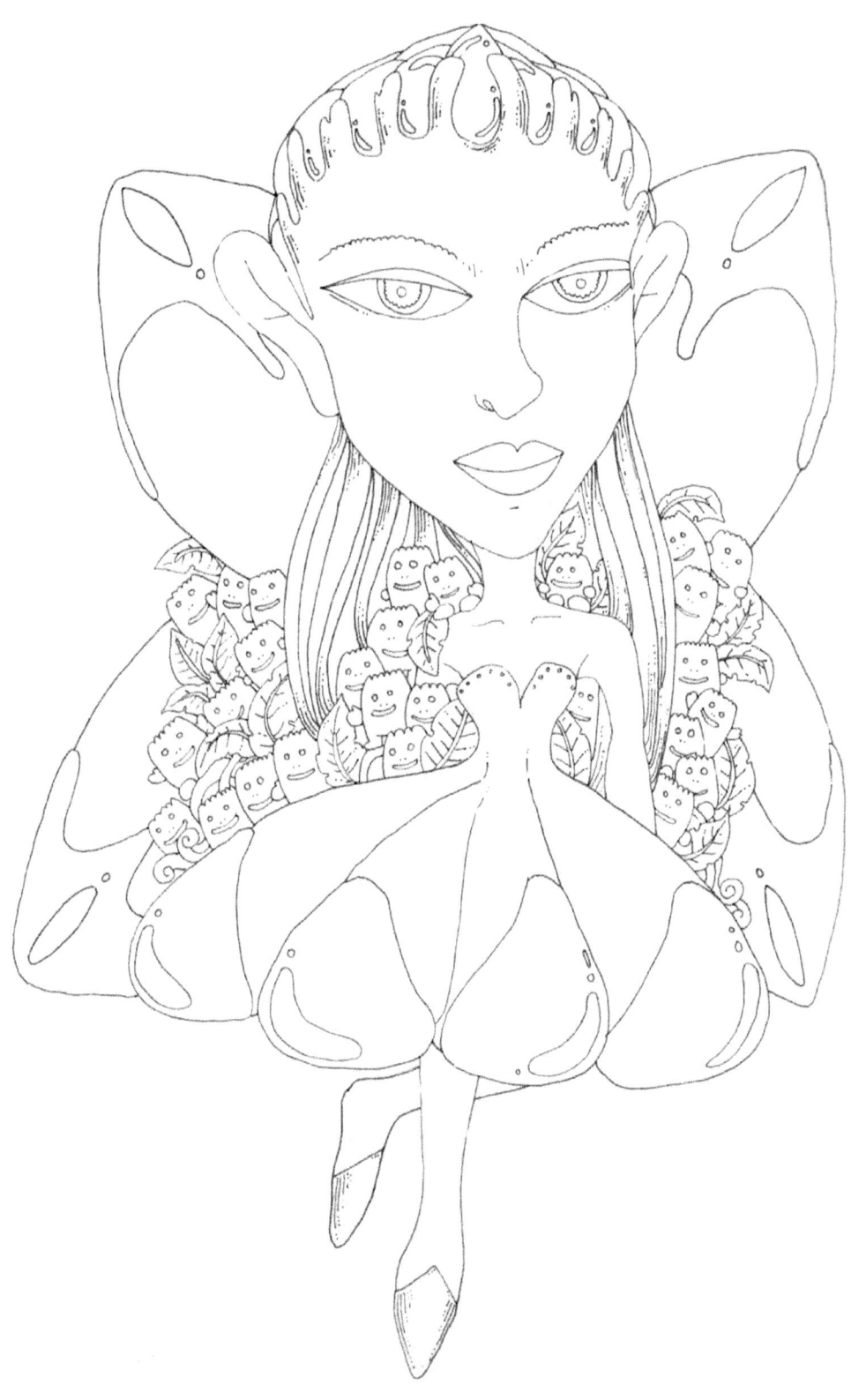

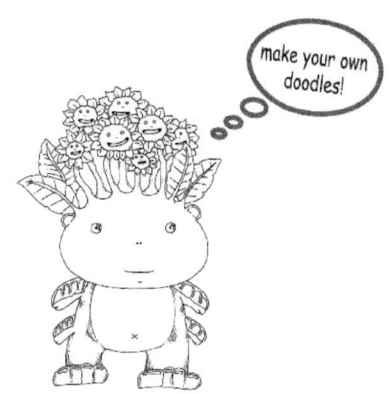

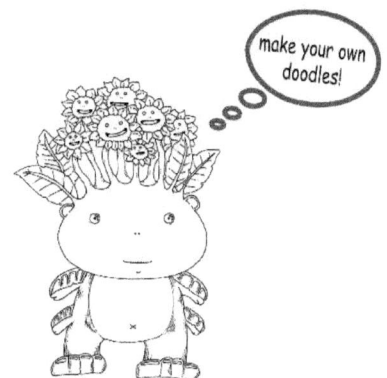

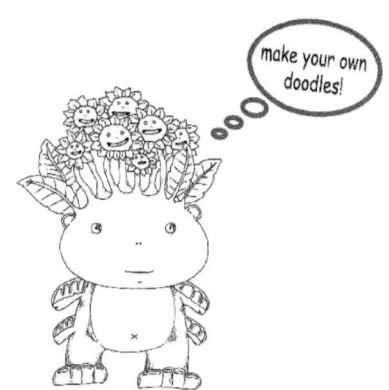

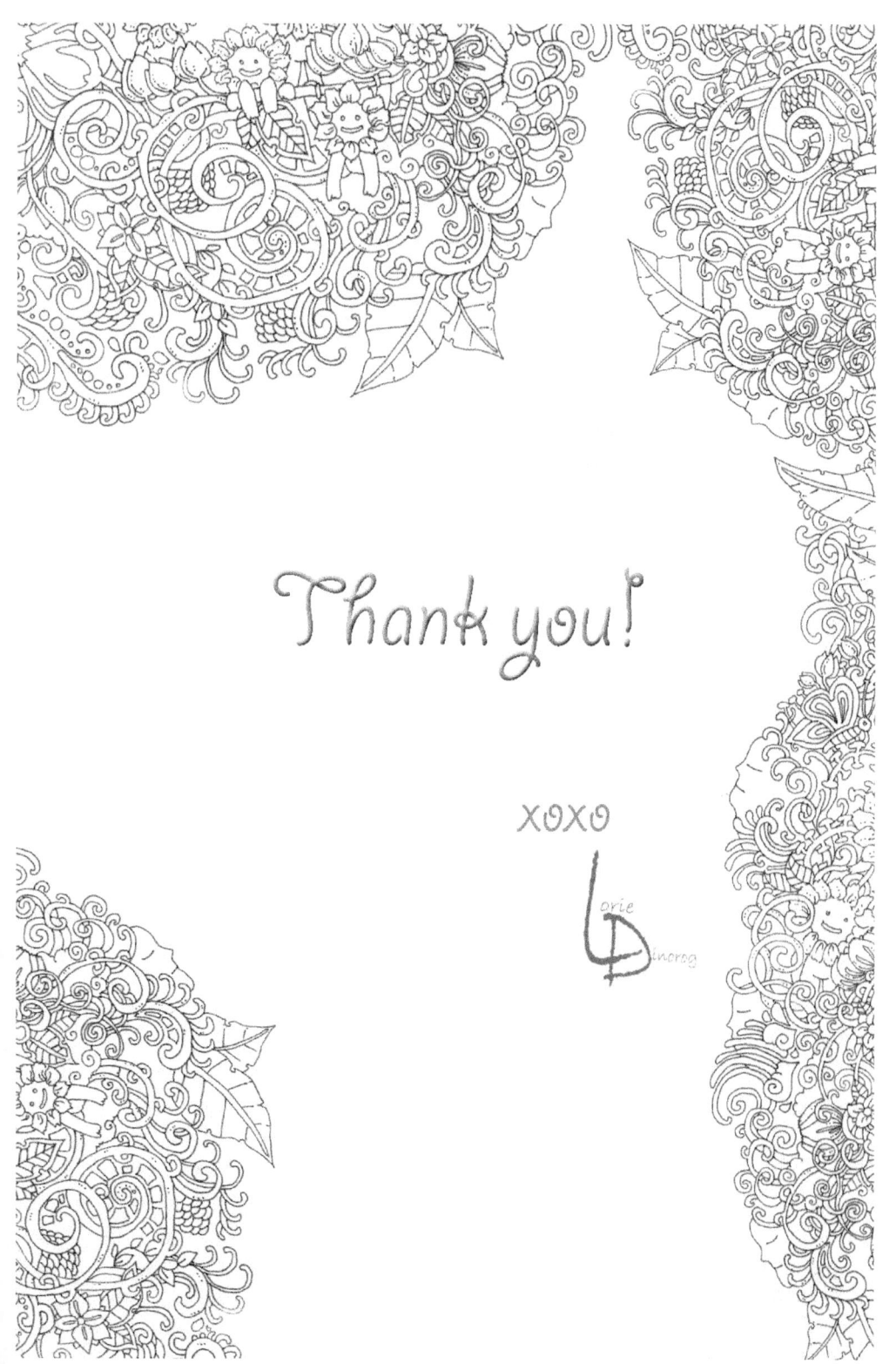

www.ingramcontent.com/pod-product-compliance
Lightning Source LLC
Chambersburg PA
CBHW070311230526
45470CB00002B/817